Teaching
Writing
With
Rubrics

To
Teachers, whose influence can alter the life of a child;
Students, whose discovery of the truly wonderful world of writing is just a rubric away;
and
Molly E. Espinoza, a former student whose love of life and flair for
writing were prematurely silenced, leaving a void in our hearts.
July 17, 1985 – April 24, 2003

I see, and I forget.
I hear, and I remember.
I do, and I understand.

—*Chinese proverb*

Teaching Writing With Rubrics

Practical Strategies and Lesson Plans for Grades 2-8

LAURA A. FLYNN ✦ ELLEN M. FLYNN

CORWIN PRESS
A Sage Publications Company
Thousand Oaks, California

For information:

Corwin Press
A Sage Publications Company
2455 Teller Road
Thousand Oaks, California 91320
www.corwinpress.com

Sage Publications Ltd.
1 Oliver's Yard
55 City Road
London EC1Y 1SP
United Kingdom

Sage Publications India Pvt. Ltd.
B-42, Panchsheel Enclave
Post Box 4109
New Delhi 110 017 India

Printed in the United States of America

Library of Congress Cataloging-in-Publication Data

Flynn, Laura A.
Teaching writing with rubrics : practical strategies and lesson
plans for grades 2-8 / by Laura A. Flynn and Ellen M. Flynn.
        p. cm.
Includes bibliographical references and index.
ISBN 0-7619-3183-X (cloth) — ISBN 0-7619-3184-8 (paper)
    1. English language—Composition and exercises—Study and teaching
(Elementary)—United States. 2. English language—Composition and
exercises—Study and teaching (Middle school)—United States.
3. English language—Composition and exercises—Study and
teaching—Evaluation. I. Flynn, Ellen M. II. Title.
LB1576.F493 2004
372.62'3044—dc22

                                        2003024349

This book is printed on acid-free paper.

04 05 06 07 10 9 8 7 6 5 4 3 2 1

Acquisitions Editor:	Kylee Liegl
Editorial Assistant:	Jaime Cuvier
Production Editor:	Kristen Gibson
Copy Editor:	Kate Peterson
Typesetter:	C&M Digitals (P) Ltd.
Cover Designer:	Michael Dubowe
Production Artist:	Lisa Miller

Contents

Foreword

*D*o you find it difficult covering all the required material for each subject? Do you struggle with trying to grade assignments quickly, objectively, and accurately? These are challenges we, as teachers, face daily. We are expected to expand our curriculum year after year, as well as provide a deeper analysis of students' work. As these tasks become increasingly arduous, we must seek out more efficient and effective methods to accomplish these duties. The demands on educators grow while the time to get the job done remains the same. Teachers want to assess their students accurately and communicate this to them in a positive and productive manner. The rubric program that Laura and Ellen Flynn have developed in their classrooms offers teachers assistance in these areas.

During the years Laura and Ellen were developing this system with their fifth-grade students, they shared their ideas with me. I saw writing assignments and projects from their students that were of a higher quality and deeper thinking level than my students were producing. I quickly put the rubrics to use in my own fifth-grade class. The components this system provided that stood out immediately to me were student accountability, parent communication, public criteria of my expectations, quick and objective grading, and a detailed report and analysis of student work. As I continued the use of this system, I found my students were also producing higher-quality and more thoughtful work as well.

I also found that one assignment could provide assessment for more than one subject. For instance, we could work on language arts and social studies through the same assignment as my students wrote a paper on a Native American group. Through the rubrics they would produce projects and present them to the class as I assessed their speaking and listening skills along with the science, social studies, or reading subject they were covering. I could grade more than one skill right then and provide immediate feedback to my students. This quick, outlined assessment was more effective and my students improved more quickly. The rubrics helped provide further instruction for them because they break down the tasks into smaller chunks that are less daunting. It was interesting that science and social studies concepts were being incorporated into their creative writing as well. Another distinguishing factor of this system is that it fit into my teaching style and situation without much alteration. I adapted their ideas easily and quickly to the needs of my students.

A personal goal I have as an educator is to help students become more involved in their own education and to be able to assess their own assignments. This rubric system lays the groundwork for students to be able to take more responsibility for their own work. This helps them to grow socially as well as academically.

Laura and Ellen Flynn have very organized programs and environments. Their students remain on task and develop into independent learners. They involve parents effectively. I have seen their interaction with students and parents. Their program is student centered, they know what students need, and the parents show great appreciation for their work. This book is a reflection of their knowledge and experience. Using their ideas for organization and grading lightened my load as a teacher. It also helped me become a better teacher. I am grateful for the time and concern they gave to me. I highly recommend this program!

LISA O'RILEY

M.A. in elementary education,
emphasis in language arts
28 years of teaching experience

Preface

*T*his book was written to provide both new and existent teachers with a practical guide and application for using the writing process. The focus in *Teaching Writing With Rubrics* is how to use rubrics to guide your students through the writing process. It is not intended to be an instructional book on what the writing process is; there are already many wonderful books available on that topic (see Resource B for a list of references). Therefore I strongly recommend that you read one or more of the books listed in Resource B to gain a better understanding of the writing process before attempting to use this book.

Teaching Writing With Rubrics is a compilation of strategies taken from the following sources: Nancie Atwell's book, *In the Middle: Writing, Reading, and Learning With Adolescents* (Boynton/Cook Publishers, 1987); New Zealand's Style of Balanced Literacy observed in an elementary school in Phoenix, Arizona, in 1996 (The Learning Network, www.rcowen. com); and the concept of "Morning Message." Ideas and suggestions from these sources were taken and put together in a form that is easy to follow and ready to use. What Ellen and I refer to as "our program" is really a combination of all these programs together, adapted to fit our purpose in the classroom.

The chapter titled "Setting Up Your Classroom Writing Program" expands on how we put theory into practice in our classrooms. What we found lacking in our undergraduate schooling, as well as in many of the research-based books, was information on how to get students to actually complete an assignment, as well as how to evaluate it once they did. The rubrics in this book are the result of years of research, planning, and experimenting. We have found a system that works; and with that in mind, we feel a need to share it with others. *Teaching Writing With Rubrics* is designed to provide you with

- Step-by-step instructions on how to set up a classroom writing program that takes students through the writing process
- Information on how to teach students to budget their time for long-term projects
- Instructions on how to use the writing process and programs such as *Six Trait Writing* to build on students' skills and improve their talent for writing

- An explanation on how to evaluate each part of the process every step of the way
- Reproducibles that are ready to use

We wish you the best of luck in discovering what your students can produce when given a rubric and challenged to do their best. You may be amazed, as we often are, by the hidden talents of many of your students.

LAURA FLYNN

Acknowledgments

There are many people who have influenced my life, and without whose love and support I would not be who I am today. At this time, I would like to thank especially the people who have helped me take this book from conception to reality.

First of all, I would like to thank my cousin, Margaret Patrick, for coming to visit at a time when I needed her as much as she needed me. She gave me the motivation I needed to continue to work on this project after putting it on the shelf for a year.

A special thank-you goes to Rob Barraclough, my undergraduate speech communications professor, for believing in me as a teacher at a time when I doubted myself, and for showing me how a dynamic teacher can influence the very heart and soul of a student.

I would also like to thank all of my family and friends who listened to my ideas and encouraged me to go on when the book was in its early stages, especially Cynthia Johnson, my sister; Ken and Maggie Johnson, my brother and sister-in-law; Marcella and Charles Johnson, my mother and father; Liz Romero, who has always been more like a sister than a friend; Melanie Donahue, whose generous heart and spirit made it possible for me to work two mornings a week without interruption from my children; and Ellen Flynn; my mother-in-law, partner, and best friend. Her influence, experience, and feedback were monumental in shaping me into the teacher that I am today, as well as in the development of this book.

Most important, I would like to thank God, St. Therese, and the power of prayer! Thank-you, also, goes to the Nanez family for their role in answering my prayers.

LAURA FLYNN

I am grateful, and truly blessed by God, for the relationship Laura and I have always had. Being a mother-in-law and daughter-in-law teaching team (in the same classroom) made us a unique pair. Our love for teaching and the challenge of reaching each one of our students, no matter the ability level, became our common thread. We spent many hours together planning our rubrics, which were the central components of all our thematic units. We called it our quality family time.

I also want to acknowledge my father, Joseph Duben, who passed away while I was starting my master's program. He was very proud of me and encouraged me by listening to me and making sure I did not skip a class while he was ill. My sisters, Mickey Fitzpatrick and Tina Gray, and my dearest friend, Susan Lazane, are always by my side with love and support, for which I owe them my unending gratitude. I also want to thank my mother, Nora Duben, and my three sons (J. J., Kelly, and Shawn) for believing in me and encouraging our endeavor to finish this book.

ELLEN FLYNN

We are both greatly indebted to Lisa O'Riley for serving as a sounding board and personal editor during the drafting of this book, for the invaluable feedback she gave us, and for using our rubrics and believing in what we had to offer.

We would also like to show our gratitude to Anne Claunch, Ph.D. and director of the UNM/APS Resident Teacher Program, for putting the idea in our minds nine years ago that what we were doing in our classrooms was something we should share with others in print form, and for providing us with the opportunity to educate the UNM Resident Teachers about our writing program, rubrics, and teaching thematically.

We are very grateful to Jack Vermillion, principal at Chelwood Elementary when we team-taught together, for giving us the opportunity to work together (even though he had his doubts on the ability of a mother-in-law and daughter-in-law to work together peaceably and effectively). We would never have become the teachers we are had he not given us the chance to team-teach together.

Thank-you also goes to Dr. Allan Holmquist, the new principal at Chelwood Elementary, for all his support and advice during contract negotiations, and for giving us the opportunity to once again work together at the same school.

There are also many parents and students in the Chelwood community to whom we owe a great deal of appreciation: the parents, for all their involvement, support, and expressions of gratitude for how our program aided their children in the transition to middle school and made a difference in their lives; and the students, for all their efforts and hard work in rising to our high expectations and for showing us the amazing quality of work even a fifth grader can produce. We would especially like to thank the following students for allowing us to use their work as examples: Carly Cloud, Molly Espinoza, Kiley Kartchner, Joel Kent, Evelynn Moore, John Perea, Laura Perea, Samantha Phelps, Victor Ramos, and Holly Twitchell.

And, of course, we would like to thank our husbands, Kelly and Jim Flynn, who never complained about all the hours we spent together while planning our units when we first started teaching. They became our "Mr. Moms" while we were taking classes, teaching, and developing our curriculum. Thank you both for your love and continued support through this book-writing process.

LAURA FLYNN AND ELLEN FLYNN

Corwin Press gratefully acknowledges the contributions of the following reviewers:

Belinda Prentice
Fourth-grade teacher
Gardendale Elementary School
Gardendale, AL

Shelley Johnson
Second-grade teacher
Lincoln Elementary School
Great Falls, MT

Introduction

When I first started teaching in the early 1990s, I had no idea how to *teach* writing. The big push in education at the time was "Writer's Workshop," but I had a hard time understanding exactly how it worked because I never saw it implemented in the classroom when I did my student teaching. As a result, I spent a lot of time reading and researching during my first few years of teaching. I was trying to find a book that would spell it all out for me and tell me exactly how to teach writing.

What I found was information on letting students pick their own topics and work at their own paces, getting students excited about writing by allowing them to write about personal experiences, and working on your own writing along with the students so that they could see you as a writer as well. It all sounded great! So I tried it. My frustration came when we had reached the end of a nine-week grading period and most of my fifth-grade students had yet to publish just one piece of writing! I was disappointed with the reality that most students, if not given a deadline, will not turn in work. I realized that students need more than just instruction on how to write; they need instruction on time management as well. I also concluded that teachers need more than just instruction on how to get students to write; they need information on how to assess the students' works and be accountable for the grades they issue.

During this time, while I was working on my master's degree and in the midst of my second year of teaching, my mother-in-law (Ellen Flynn) was doing her student teaching. She was working in a school that had a wonderful program with innovative ideas for the classroom. We worked together, combining what she learned about using rubrics with what I learned about teaching writing. What we came up with was a plan for writing that took students through a five-part process in a three- to five-week period of time. With a rubric as a guide, students were given direction, structure, due dates, and a grading system for their writing assignments; yet they were still allowed some choice in selecting particular topics focused on a specific genre. This gave students plenty of room for creativity while also providing them with the form and framework so desperately needed to become successful life-long writers and learners. Students were challenged to work to their full potentials and abilities, which allowed us to work with the wide range of skills found in any classroom. They also became very proud of their finished products, which they presented not only to the teacher but to their peers in the classroom as well.

Teaching Writing With Rubrics bridges the gap between theory and practice. It provides the classroom teacher with the instructions, time guidelines, rubric assessments, and blackline masters needed to turn the process into a finished product. What I was looking for when I started my career as a teacher is what we are publishing now. We hope you find what you are looking for in the pages of this book.

LAURA FLYNN

About the Authors

Laura A. Flynn received her B.S. and M.A. degrees in elementary education from the University of New Mexico, where she has also served as a consultant for the Resident Teacher Program regarding the use of rubrics in the classroom and teaching thematically. She received her Instructional Leader License in 1995 and is state certified in New Mexico to teach Grades K–12. Her passions for teaching have always focused on writing, math, and teaching thematically.

Laura has been married to her husband, Kelly, for eleven years, and they have three young children: Keith, Lorren, and Justin. After Keith was born in 1997, she remained involved in education by working part time as a substitute teacher for the Albuquerque Public Schools. When the twins arrived in 2000, she limited her time teaching to six weeks out of the year at the Albuquerque Academy's Summer Enrichment Program in Albuquerque, New Mexico. She has recently returned to the Albuquerque Public Schools to work part time at Chelwood Elementary as an Instructional Coach (supporting teachers in their methods of instruction).

Ellen M. Flynn received her B.S. and M.A. degrees in elementary education from the University of New Mexico. She has given presentations through the University of New Mexico and the College of Santa Fe, to both current and future teachers, about thematic planning and using rubrics for writing, reading, special projects, cooperative learning labs, and math. She currently teaches a fourth- and fifth-grade combination class at Chelwood Elementary in Albuquerque, New Mexico. Ellen is responsible for training all the fourth- and fifth-grade students in conflict mediation at her school. She is also involved with the school's Instructional Council and the Tech Integration Team, and she was part of the Support Team for many years.

Ellen has been married to her husband, Jim, for thirty-five years. They have three grown sons and seven grandchildren, who are the rays of sunshine in their lives. When they are not working or playing with their grandchildren, they are busy traveling and discovering their roots in Ireland.

PART I
Getting Started

1

About Rubrics

WHAT IS A RUBRIC?

A rubric is a form of assessment that evaluates a student's work on a numbered scale. Students are assigned a numbered point that is indicative of the quality of their work. The description assigned to a number can vary from being very detailed and specific to very simple as in the example below:

1	2	3	4	5
poor	below average	average	above average	excellent

When using a scale of 1 to 10, think percentagewise when evaluating a student's work. For example:

6 = 60%	7 = 70%	8 = 80%	9 = 90%	10 = 100%

HOW WE USED RUBRICS
IN OUR WRITING PROGRAM

Throughout the course of this text, we use the term "rubric" interchangeably with "contract" or "assignment." When we refer to "our rubrics," we are referring to the blackline masters of the student contracts. Our rubrics are set up so that each assignment is worth a total of 100 points or a multiple thereof. This facilitates in assigning a letter grade to the finished product. Those points are then broken down and assigned to each part of the writing process. For example:

Pre-writing	5 points
Rough draft	50 points
Final draft	40 points
Presentation	5 points
Total	100 points

Each part of the writing process is then broken down even further to state specifically what each point is for. For example, if the final draft is worth 40 points, those points might be broken down as follows:

a. Used correct spelling, punctuation, and grammar (10 points)

b. Corrections from conference were made (10 points)

c. Followed the correct format (10 points)

d. Neatness and care were taken in publication (10 points)

We developed all the writing rubrics in this book to go along with thematic units we were teaching in our fifth-grade classrooms. Although each assignment focuses on a particular theme, each one can easily be modified to meet your individual classroom needs. We have included information with each rubric elaborating on how you might modify the assignment. Once you become familiar with the format of our rubrics, you may feel comfortable designing your own to better meet your teaching style, interests, or students' needs. We have also included a section at the back of the book to help guide you through this.

Also, we feel it is important to state that this was not the only form of "English" instruction going on in our classrooms. Textbooks were used primarily as reference materials, but our mornings started with what we have termed our *ASAP Time* (*Assignments, Skills, And Proofreading*) (see Chapter 2). Time was also spent during one unit outlining a section in our text that focused on how to use the writing process, as well as many elements of writing, to become a better writer (see Chapter 2). We believe it was all of these components used together that added to the improvement and growth we saw among our students throughout the course of a school year.

A major advantage in using our program is that every individual student's needs are met. A teacher is always faced with a wide range of abilities in any classroom, from students who perform far below grade level to those who excel well beyond. Unlike worksheets or "story starters," with the use of these rubrics, students are challenged to put what they know about writing to use. With every assignment, students build on their knowledge and learn new skills that are appropriate and apply to the purpose of *their* writing. It becomes a yearlong process that builds with each new assignment.

WHY USE RUBRICS?

Once you have the experience of working with rubrics, you may wonder how you ever got along without them. There are many good reasons to teach using this tool. Below is an outline and explanation of how rubrics can benefit both you and your students in the classroom.

- Ensure teacher and student accountability
- State your expectations
- Reduce teacher subjectivity
- Ensure that the writing curriculum is met

Ensure Teacher and Student Accountability

Teacher accountability is a growing factor in all school districts these days. How to be accountable for the curriculum you are teaching, as well as how to grade students and be accountable for the grades you issue, are covered with the use of our rubrics. The rubric itself is a tool that explains at a glance what you are teaching, your pedagogy, and how the students will be graded.

Student accountability for an assignment is also an important issue. As teachers, many times we do too much for the students, taking on many of their responsibilities. With the use of a rubric, students are held accountable for their work. They know exactly what is expected, when parts are due, and how they will be graded. It then becomes the *student's* responsibility to ensure that all requirements for the assignment are met.

Our rubrics are set up in the form of a contract where a student's signature is required for each assignment. We have found it especially helpful in the elementary grades to require a parent signature as well. This ensures that the parents are also aware of what their child's specific responsibilities are. We have therefore provided you with both options in our reproducible pages.

State Your Expectations

With the use of a rubric, there are no surprises for the students. Everything that is required is spelled out, and students know exactly how they will be graded. Excuses such as "I didn't know . . ." or "You never said . . ." are eliminated because the expectations are written, and students are encouraged to refer back to them. By stating your public criteria in contract form, there is never any question about what is expected from the students.

Reduce Teacher Subjectivity

One of the hardest parts of grading any writing project is trying to remain objective. With the use of a rubric, it is much easier to do so because the assignment is broken down into smaller, more manageable parts. It is stated exactly how points are to be issued for each part of the project. As a result, teacher subjectivity is virtually eliminated.

Ensure That the Writing Standards Are Met

Each state is governed by a set of National Standards for education. Each school district, in turn, is governed by its own state's standards. Listed below are some of the National Standards that are covered using our rubrics.

National Standards for Language Arts (2002)

- Students adjust their use of spoken, written, and visual language (e.g., conventions, style, vocabulary) to communicate effectively with a variety of audiences and for different purposes.
- Students employ a wide range of strategies as they write and use different writing process elements appropriately to communicate with different audiences for a variety of purposes.
- Students apply knowledge of language structure, language conventions (e.g., spelling and punctuation), media techniques, figurative language, and genre to create, critique, and discuss print and nonprint texts.
- Students conduct research on issues and interests by generating ideas and questions, and by posing problems. They gather, evaluate, and synthesize data from a variety of sources (e.g., print and nonprint texts, artifacts, people) to communicate their discoveries in ways that suit their purpose and audience.
- Students use a variety of technological and informational resources (e.g., libraries, databases, computer networks, video) to gather and synthesize information and to create and communicate knowledge.
- Students whose first language is not English make use of their first language to develop competency in the English language arts and to develop understanding of content across the curriculum.
- Students participate as knowledgeable, reflective, creative, and critical members of a variety of literacy communities.
- Students use spoken, written, and visual language to accomplish their own purposes (e.g., for learning, enjoyment, persuasion, and the exchange of information).

Meeting Your School District's Standards

As we developed these writing rubrics, we planned backwards. We studied the curriculum standards that were required in our school district and created our writing rubrics to meet those needs. Throughout the course of the year, using the variety of assignments included in this book (along with our reading program and poetry unit), all standards were covered and met.

One of our most important jobs, as educators, is to know our district's standards and to develop a curriculum that meets them. Using the rubrics included in this book, most writing standards will be met. We do advise you, however, to examine your school district's standards and adapt the rubrics as needed. Please refer to Chapter 15, "How to Create Your Own Rubrics," for more information on how to do this.

2

Setting Up Your Classroom Writing Program

An important aspect of our writing program is the way that we incorporated instruction on time management and organization into our daily classroom routine. Teaching kids how to budget their time for long-term projects is not an easy task. As teachers, many times we expect our students to know how to do this, but all too often it is not a skill they have ever been taught. How many students have you known who waited until the day before an assignment was due to even begin the project? Time management and organization are just like any other skills; students have to be taught *how* to use them in order to implement them properly.

We have found there are four key elements to teaching students about time management and organization: assignment books, a daily assignment board, calendars (with due dates color coded by subject), and a structured, organized classroom routine.

7

Student Planners, Agendas, or Assignment Books

We cannot emphasize enough the importance of having students use assignment books in the classroom. We required students to have a planner that not only had places to record daily assignments but had at-a-glance monthly calendars as well. This requirement was key in teaching students how to budget their time for long-term projects, as we explain in the next two sections. For a list of possible resources from which to order these, see Resource B.

Keys to Teaching Time Management to Students

- Student planners, agendas, or assignment books
- A daily assignment board
- Calendars
- A structured and organized classroom routine

A Daily Assignment Board

In the front of our classrooms, we kept a white board posted that stated the assignments for the day as well as a reminder of when any long-term projects were due. Teaching in elementary school, our assignment boards displayed the assignments for each subject. Many times there were several projects going on at once, which made the use of a planner and calendar even more important.

One of the students' first priorities when they walked into the classroom was to take out their planners and copy down the day's assignments from the assignment board. Once they were done, they were required to leave their books out and open on a corner of their desk. This way, not only could we tell when they had finished this task, but once they finished an assignment, they could easily check it off as being completed. Requiring the students to do this every day reinforced good study skills.

Figure 2.1   Sample Assignment Board

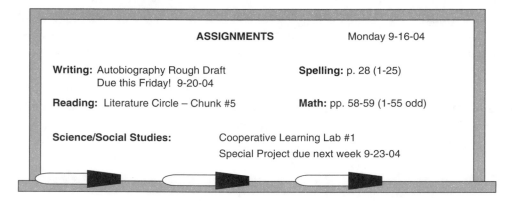

Calendars

Whenever we introduced a writing assignment, students were responsible for not only filling in the due dates on the spaces provided on the rubric, but we also had them fill in all the due dates on the calendar in their assignment books as well. We used an overhead (made from a calendar found in one of the student planners) to model this for the students, and taught them to use a color code to easily distinguish among the assignments for the different subjects. For example, Writing assignments were written in blue, Reading was written in green, Cooperative Learning Labs and Special Projects dealing with our social studies or science units in red, and so on. Seeing the due dates on the calendar in this way made it easier for students to visualize and prioritize their time with other family, extracurricular, or school obligations.

Other ways we incorporated the use of calendars was by using the front bulletin board (near our assignment board) to post a large one with all the due dates (color coded by subject), any holidays, or special school events noted. Students were also encouraged to keep a calendar at home near the quiet place where they studied to help reinforce good study habits and project awareness.

One advantage to teaching all subjects in the classroom was that we were able to plan projects so students did not have several assignments

Figure 2.2   Sample Calendar

Sun.	Mon.	Tues.	Wed.	Thurs.	Fri.	Sat.
1	2	3	4	5	6	7
8	Introduce 9 Writing **Introduce Reading**	10 **Chunk 1**	11 **Chunk 2** *Introduce Special Project*	Pre-write 12 due! **Chunk 3**	13 **Chunk 4** *Introduce Co-op Labs*	14
15	16 **Chunk 5** *Lab 1*	17 **Chunk 6** *Lab 2*	18 **Chunk 7**	19 **Chunk 8** *Lab 3*	Rough 20 Draft due! **Chunk 9** *Lab 4*	21
22	23 Conferences **Chunk 10** *Lab 5*	24 ◄— *Special Project Presentations* **Reading Journal Due!** *Lab 6*	25 *all week —►*	26 **Reading Project Due!**	Final 27 Draft due! Presentations Unit Wrap-up!	28
29	30					

due on the same day. We always emphasized, however, that once students reached middle school, they might not be so lucky. We continually stressed the importance of good study habits, and the use of this method to track their assignments, throughout middle school and high school.

A Structured and Organized Classroom Routine

Another important step in teaching these skills to students is to have your classroom set up in an organized manner and to have structure built into your daily routine. Teaching in elementary school, we were able to schedule at least an hour for writing each day. Whatever your circumstances may be, we highly recommend that the amount of class time spent on writing should be *at least* 45 minutes a day, five days a week. We divided our class time up into two parts. We spent about 15 minutes at the beginning of class on what we termed our *ASAP Time* (*Assignments, Skills, And Proofreading*). The remaining 45 minutes were spent on *Process Writing Time* using the rubric assignments.

ASAP Time (10-15 minutes)

- Assignments:
  - Copy the assignments from the assignment board
- Skills:
  - Students copy and edit a passage on the board for grammar, spelling, and mechanics
  - Teach mini-lessons (*Six Trait Writing*)
  - Give students practice for standardized testing
- Proofreading:
  - Model proofreading and editing skills daily

Process Writing Time (35-45 minutes)

- Work on the rubric assignments

ASAP Time (10-15 minutes)

When students walked into our classrooms, they knew exactly what was expected of them. After copying the assignments into their assignment books, their next priority was to copy a passage written on the blackboard into their spiral notebooks. What we had written on the board varied from a sentence or two to a paragraph or an address, with several mistakes in grammar, spelling, or mechanics. The students were required to copy this passage exactly as it was written, errors and all. We expected them to skip lines when writing these in order to leave room to correct the mistakes using their red pens and proofreading marks. A list of resources for this activity can be found in Resource B.

Once everyone had copied and edited the passage on the board, we had time to go over how many mistakes they found, what they were, and

Figure 2.3   Sample Skills Sentences

(as written on the board)

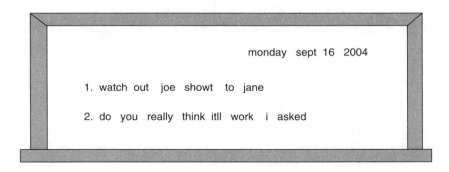

monday   sept 16   2004

1. watch out   joe   showt   to   jane

2. do   you   really   think   itll   work   i   asked

(after corrections are made)

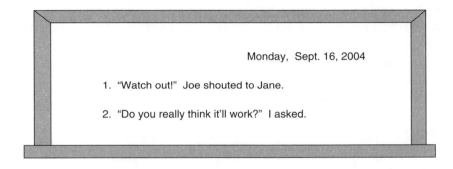

Monday,   Sept. 16, 2004

1. "Watch out!" Joe shouted to Jane.

2. "Do you really think it'll work?" I asked.

In the above example, we were able to cover the following skills:

Punctuation:	As used in dates	**Capitalization:**	With proper nouns
	When abbreviating		At the beginning of a sentence
	With quotations		When using "I" alone
	With contractions		
	Of sentence types (exclamatory, declarative, interrogative)		
Grammar:	Subject/verb tense agreement		

why they were wrong. During this time we were able to cover aspects of writing and grammar such as sentence type, figures of speech, spelling, verb tense and agreement, parts of speech, punctuation, capitalization, and many other conventions of writing, not to mention that we were reinforcing daily the proper use of editing and proofreading skills.

We sometimes used this time to teach mini-lessons focused on the skills that we saw students needing to develop more in their writing. We would do this using "anonymous" excerpts from some of our students' own composition books. If you use *Six Trait Writing*, this would be an ideal time for instructing students on the traits. We have even used this time to prepare students for standardized testing, using practice booklets.

However you choose to use this time, it is important to remain consistent with your expectations of the students. Our students understood that they were expected to come in quietly to complete the task at hand, and many students enjoyed the challenge of accurately finding and correcting the mistakes in the passage on the board.

Process Writing Time (35–45 minutes)

Our next block of class time was allotted for work on the rubric assignments. Students always knew what part of the process they were working on because it was written on the assignment board along with a reminder of the due date. Your role in the classroom during this time is primarily as facilitator. Students work independently on the assignment, which gives you the opportunity to work with students as needed. You could also use this time to work on your own writing as a model for the students.

In setting up our class time in this structured and organized manner, students always knew what to expect. We reinforced good study habits while teaching them the elemental skills necessary for employing good writing techniques.

SUPPLIES

Below is a list of supplies we required the students to have, followed by an explanation of how they were used in the classroom:

- Student planner or assignment book
- Spiral notebook
- Bound composition book
- Copies of the following (see Resource A):
  - Composition Book Guidelines
  - Proofreading Marks
  - Editing Checklist
  - Table of Contents
  - "Skills I Have Learned" list
- Pencils, black or blue ink pens
- Red pens
- Folder with pockets

Student Planner or Assignment Book

This requirement was key in teaching students about time management and organization, as we discussed in the previous section. To make sure that students had the kind of assignment books we required, we special ordered them and had them available for parents to buy at registration. See Resource B for a list of possible resources.

Spiral Notebook

We had the students use spiral notebooks for recording their daily board work during our ASAP Time. This was how we taught grammar, editing, and proofreading skills. In addition to using different books (see Appendix B for a list of resources), we frequently made up our own sentences as well, depending on our needs or those of our students.

Bound Composition Book

We required that students use standard, black, bound composition books for all of their pre-writings and rough drafts. These can be found in any office supply store. Just as we did with the assignment books, we would often purchase these prior to registration to have them available for parents at that time. We did this to ensure that students had the proper type of book we required for our program.

Copies of the Following (see Resource A)

An explanation of how to use these is found later in this chapter:

- Composition Book Guidelines
- Proofreading Marks
- Editing Checklist
- Table of Contents
- "Skills I Have Learned" list

Pencils, Black or Blue Ink Pens

These were required for the pre-writings, rough drafts, and final drafts. Requiring lead, black, or blue ink eliminated the rainbow of colors you might otherwise find students using. This made it easier to determine which writing was the "draft" writing and which was the "editing" writing.

Red Pens

We required that students use these when editing and proofreading their work. Red ink made it easier to see how much the students actually edited prior to turning in their rough drafts.

Folder With Pockets

Students kept their copies of the rubrics, supplementary handouts, and materials needed for research or their final drafts in this Writing Folder.

HOW TO HAVE STUDENTS
SET UP THEIR COMPOSITION BOOKS

We found a composition book to be the best choice for the students' pre-writings and rough drafts. This is used as a portfolio of the student's work from the beginning of the school year until the end. Pages are never removed (if using a spiral notebook, students are tempted to tear out pages). In keeping the book intact, it is also easy to see how each student's writing has grown and improved from the beginning of the year to the end. Students are often amazed at the end of the year when they can look back and see their own development as a writer.

The composition book should be set up as follows, using the reproducible pages found in Resource A:

- A copy of the Composition Book Guidelines is placed in the front of the book on the inside cover.
- On the front of the first page of the composition book, students should attach the Proofreading Marks.
- On the back of the first page should be the Editing Checklist.
- The front of the second page should be set up for the Table of Contents.
- A copy of the "Skills I Have Learned" list is placed in the back of the book on the inside cover.
- The remaining pages are available for the students to use for their pre-writings and rough drafts.

(See Figures 2.4, 2.5, and 2.6.)

Figure 2.4

Front of book (inside cover)	Front of first page

Composition Book Guidelines	**Proofreading Marks**	
* Put the date on each assignment (pre-write and rough draft)	Begin a new paragraph or indent the paragraph.	Once upon a time...
* Keep your Table of Contents updated	Insert a letter, word, phrase, or sentence.	was He named George.
* Identify your **G**enre, **A**udience, **S**ubject (topic), and **P**urpose (**GASP**) on your pre-write and rough draft	Insert a comma.	We took coats hats, and mittens with us.
* Write in pencil, blue or black ink only	Insert quotation marks.	Stop! Shouted Sam.
* Skip lines on your rough draft	Insert a period.	This is my project .
* Write legibly	Take out a letter, word, phrase, or sentence.	I made a a mistake.
* Self-edit using your Editing Checklist and Proofreading Marks.	Change a capital letter to a small letter.	He went to School.
* Use a red pen only when editing your work.	Change a small letter to a capital letter.	We saw karen.
* Make corrections in red ink only	Check the spelling of a word.	Plese edit your draft.
* Do not erase, simply cross out mistakes		
* Keep all pages intact		

Figure 2.5

Back of first page	Front of second page

Editing Checklist	**Table of Contents**
- Did I review my "Skills I Have Learned" list in the back of my composition book? - Did I follow all the Composition Book Guidelines? - Did I indent all my paragraphs? - Did I spell all words correctly? - Did I begin each sentence with a capital letter? - Did I end each sentence with the correct punctuation? - Did I use commas, apostrophes, quotation marks, and other punctuation correctly? - Did I include a topic sentence and supporting details? - Was each sentence a complete thought? - Did I read my paper aloud to myself for clarity and variety?	1._____ 2._____ 3._____ 4._____ 5._____ 6._____ 7._____ 8._____ 9._____ 10._____ 11._____ 12._____ 13._____ 14._____ 15._____

Figure 2.6

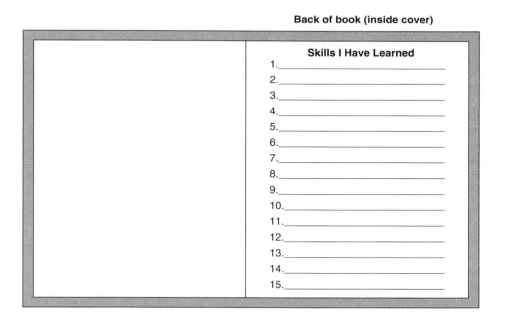

	Back of book (inside cover)
	Skills I Have Learned
	1._____ 2._____ 3._____ 4._____ 5._____ 6._____ 7._____ 8._____ 9._____ 10._____ 11._____ 12._____ 13._____ 14._____ 15._____

USING THE WRITING PROCESS

The following section expands on how we implemented the writing process in our classrooms using rubrics. We are assuming you have some background knowledge about the writing process, and therefore we will not go into great detail about what it is and all the ways it can be used. Instead, we will focus solely on how the rubrics can be used to guide your students through the process.

Steps in the Writing Process

Pre-writing
Rough draft
Conferencing
Final draft/publication
Presentation

Pre-writing

Most of our assignments lend themselves well to having students either cluster or outline their pre-writings. The type of graphic organizer that students choose to use is not important. What is important is how well they portray to you what will be included in their rough drafts. The pre-writing plans the students create should give you a clear idea as to how well they understand the assignment, as well as whether or not they will be including all the requirements in their drafts.

There are a few expectations we have from students regarding their pre-writings. First of all, they must be written in the composition books prior to the rough drafts. This makes it easy for the students to refer back to them when drafting their assignments. Also, as stated in the Composition Book Guidelines, the students must include the date as well as the *Genre, Audience, Subject* (topic), and *Purpose* (*GASP*) with their pre-writing plans. Having students write out the GASP helps them keep in mind the purpose of their writing as well as the voice and language they might use for the intended audience when drafting their assignments.

Examples of what a cluster and outline pre-writing might look like for the persuasive essay assignment can be found in Figure 2.7 and on the following page.

Persuasive Essay: Outline Example

G–Essay

A–Peers and adults

S–Country Western dancing

P–To persuade

I. Country Western dancing
   A. Easy to learn
   B. Great source of exercise
   C. Fun!

Figure 2.7   Persuasive Essay: Cluster Example

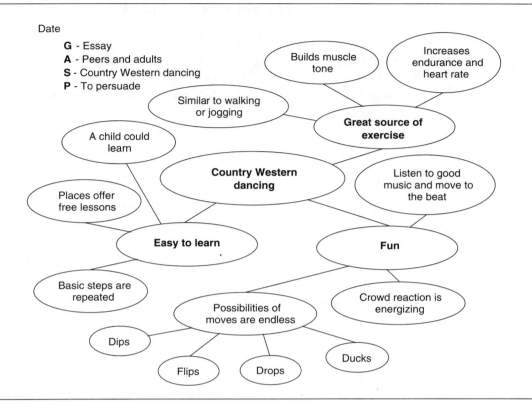

II. Easy to learn
   A. Places offer free lessons
   B. So simple, a child could learn
   C. Basic steps are repeated

III. Great source of exercise
   A. Similar to walking or jogging
   B. Increases endurance and heart rate
   C. Builds muscle tone

IV. Fun!
   A. Possibilities of moves are endless
      1. Dips
      2. Flips
      3. Drops
      4. Ducks
   B. Listen to good music and move to the beat
   C. Crowd reaction is energizing

V. Country Western dancing
   A. Easy to learn
   B. Great source of exercise
   C. Fun!

The pre-writing should

- be in the form of a graphic organizer (i.e., cluster, outline, etc.).
- demonstrate that the student understands the assignment.
- be written in the composition book.
- include the date and the GASP (Genre, Audience, Subject, and Purpose).

Rough Draft

The rough draft portion of the assignment must also be written in the composition book. The Composition Book Guidelines that are placed in the front of the students' books state what we expect from them as they draft their work. Below is an explanation of what we expect, and why.

Put the Date on Each Assignment (Pre-write and Rough Draft)

As we mentioned earlier, the composition book works as a portfolio of the students' work from the beginning of the year until the end. Keeping the date on each piece makes it easier to determine when something was written while looking back through the book.

Keep Your Table of Contents Updated

This lets you know at a glance what the student has written and the order they are written in.

Identify Your Genre, Audience, Subject (Topic), and Purpose (GASP) on Your Pre-write and Rough Draft

This is required to help the students keep these things in mind while working on the assignment.

Write in Pencil, Blue or Black Ink Only

In requiring this, students are prevented from writing their rough drafts with pens that have ink colors of every shade or hue of the rainbow. It keeps it easy to tell which part is the student's original writing.

Skip Lines on Your Rough Draft

This makes it easier for students to make changes while editing. If students do not skip lines, their rough drafts can become too crowded to understand once they start to make changes. In skipping lines, students have plenty of room to add or change things. We found it helpful, during their first assignment, to have students put a mark on every other line of the page to help them remember to do this.

Write Legibly

This requirement is to make your life easier. As the teacher and final editor, it helps if you can actually read the student's writing.

Self-edit Using Your Editing Checklist and Proofreading Marks and Use a Red Pen Only When Editing Your Work

This requirement makes it essential for students to look critically at their own writing. The Editing Checklist guides them in what to look for, while the Proofreading Marks show them how to make those corrections.

Making the corrections in red ink makes it easy to see what changes the student made while editing.

Do Not Erase, Simply Cross Out Mistakes

Having students cross out their mistakes, instead of erasing them, can help you see their thought processes while writing. Actually, my preference is that students use pens for their rough drafts, because then they have to cross out their mistakes and do not have the choice of erasing.

Keep All Pages Intact

Expecting this from students keeps the book intact and helps students monitor their own development.

These are the guidelines required for *all* rough drafts. It is the basic format used regardless of the genre of the assignment. If a student does not follow them, points are deducted from the grade on this portion of the assignment. You may also notice that in the first assignment (autobiography or biography), whether or not a student follows these guidelines is worth more than in any other assignment. We did this intentionally to emphasize their importance during that first assignment when students are learning what you expect. Any guideline they do not follow could be added to their skills list in the back of the composition book.

Each rubric will also state any other requirements expected for that particular rough draft. It might state how many paragraphs it should contain, how many words it should have, or what kind of format is required.

The rough draft should be written

- in the composition book.
- according to the Composition Book Guidelines.
- according to the requirements stated on the rubric.

Conferencing

Although no points are assigned for the conference, it is essential that students participate in this prior to working on their final drafts. Once a child has turned in a rough draft, it is your responsibility to do the final editing. When doing this, look for skills the child has done well, as well as one or two skills he or she needs to work on. This is the point where instruction takes place based on the child's ability.

In Resource A, you will find a sheet titled "Skills _____ has learned." It is on this sheet that you will make anecdotal notes about the student's writing. This is for your record and accountability. It is also helpful to have this available to show parents if they are concerned at any time about how their child is doing in writing. An example of what your sheet might look like is the following:

Skills _____ Jane Doe _____ has learned

Date/Title/Genre	Skills Used Well	Skills Learned
09-20-04 Country Western dancing Persuasive essay	– Indented paragraphs. – Good use of punctuation and capitalization. – Used topic sentences and supporting details appropriately.	– Use a variety of sentence starters. – Develop transitions between paragraphs.

What you write in the "Skills Learned" column, you would also write on the student's "Skills I Have Learned" list in the back of the composition book. These are the items the student needs to improve on for publication.

Essentially, the "skills" that you focus on with each student are the "traits" of writing. This is the point where you focus your instruction based on the student's background and knowledge of writing. With some students, your focus might be primarily on conventions or organization, while with others, you may focus on more complex instruction on voice, word choice, or fluency. Taking these traits and applying them to their *own written words* makes more sense *to them* than editing a paragraph from a book, a worksheet, or even someone else's work.

It is important to remember that you should not write more than two skills for the student to work on per assignment. Remember, this is a year-long process. If a child can master just one or two skills per assignment, by the end of the year his or her writing *will* be greatly improved. The key is in having the student review that list when editing the next assignment to make sure he or she has applied those skills there as well. In requiring this, students learn from their mistakes, and skills become practical.

How you conference is up to you. Ellen and I differed in our styles for this. I preferred to have all the rough drafts graded and notes made prior to conferencing with the students. Ellen found it easier to grade the rough draft with the student sitting next to her and reading over it together. How you choose to do this is not important; do what works best for you. What is important is that during a conference you go over the grade the student received and why; take the time to explain what the student did well, along with one or two skills that must be developed for the final draft; and keep track of those skills on your "Skills _____ has learned" sheet, but record only those that the student needs to improve on in the student's composition book.

The following should be covered during the conference:

- Go over the grade the student received and why.
- Explain what the student did well.
- Go over one to two skills that the student must develop in order to improve his or her writing for the final draft.
- Make notes on your student skills sheet as well as on the student's.

Final Draft/Publication

Every assignment the students work on must be published in some form of final draft. Each rubric states specifically how that particular assignment should be finalized. Some assignments are more easily published into a class book, whereas for other assignments, the students are held responsible for setting them up in a book format. We have never found it necessary to teach students how to "bind" their books. Many either already knew or they learned from others in the class. It could be helpful, however, to have a resource book in the classroom demonstrating different binding or book-making ideas (see Resource B for a list of possible resources). In giving students the freedom to bind their books as they choose, you may be surprised by the creative finished products they turn in. The results are as varied as the students who produce them.

Regardless of the assignment, certain things are required of *all* final drafts. They must include correct spelling, punctuation, and grammar. They should always be neatly handwritten or typed. And, most important, any corrections that were discussed during the conference *must* be made in the published final draft. Requiring the latter prevents students from turning in a final draft that looks exactly like the rough draft. If a child does not make the changes discussed in the conference, learning has not taken place, and points should be deducted from the final draft.

The final draft should

- be published according to the requirements stated on the rubric.
- include correct spelling, punctuation, and grammar.
- be neatly handwritten or typed.
- include the corrections discussed during the conference.

Presentation

Students are always required to present their final drafts to the class. We believe there are several good reasons for doing this. It gives students good experience with public speaking skills, they tend to work harder on their assignments, and it gives them a feeling of success to receive positive feedback from their peers.

First of all, it gives students good experience with public speaking skills. There are five elements we look for during a presentation that are key to good public speaking: eye contact, volume, clarity, posture, and pride.

Eye Contact. The student must look at the audience intermittently when presenting; this requirement prevents students from hiding behind their work.

Volume. The student must speak in a voice loud enough for everyone to hear.

Clarity. The student should not rush the presentation, but speak in a clear voice that everyone can understand.

Posture. The student should stand straight and tall; no wiggling or slouching.

Pride. The student should sound proud of his or her work.

The presentation is always worth 5 points. That breaks down to 1 point for each element that the student implements properly.

Another good reason to have students present is that they tend to take more care and interest in writing something that they know will be presented in front of their peers and not just the teacher. For this reason, it is very important to create a classroom environment in which the kids feel safe. The first time a student presents to the class can be a terrifying situation for some students. At the beginning of the school year, we often give the kids the choice of having a friend come up with them when they present if they need that added comfort or support. Usually, it only takes one time before the kids are comfortable enough to do it on their own.

We also emphasized the importance of being a courteous and noncritical audience. Students were given the chance to give specific praise to the presenters for what they did well after each presentation. By specific we mean, "I liked the descriptive language you used in your story" or "I loved the detail in your illustrations," not just, "I liked your story" or "I liked your pictures." Giving the students a chance to hear positive praise from their peers makes getting up in front of the class much more enjoyable and less threatening. We do, however, recommend setting a limit to the number of students they can call on for praise. Otherwise, it takes too long to get through all the presentations.

The presentation is required to

- instruct students on public speaking skills (eye contact, volume, clarity, posture, and pride).
- give students the opportunity to share their work with their peers.
- instruct students on how to be a courteous and noncritical audience by praising their peers for work done well.

WHAT TO DO WITH STUDENTS WHO TURN WORK IN EARLY OR LATE

Just as any classroom is filled with students who range in their abilities, it will also be filled with students who range in their motivation as well. It seems teachers are always struggling with what to do with students who finish their work early or turn it in late. Of the students who turn their work in early, we have typically found that there are two types: those that are very intelligent, highly motivated, and turn in a high-quality product, and those who simply want to get the assignment over with, turned in, and are not necessarily concerned about the quality of their work. Then, of course, you have the handful of students who either never turn in their work on time or simply do not turn it in at all.

Of the students who turn their work in early, the former is the type of student who can become bored in a regular classroom. We are proud to say that in all the years we have been teaching, and with the wide range of students found in our classrooms every year, we have yet to have a parent or child complain of boredom with our program.

So, what do you do with a child who finishes the pre-write a day early, and the rough draft two or three days before it is due? You take advantage of it. Grade that student's work early and let him or her get started on the next part of the process. The first students to turn in their work and conference with you over their rough drafts are the first students to have access to the classroom computers to begin work on their final drafts (which, in elementary school, would often take longer than having them hand write it). These are the types of students who take pride in their work, and will usually spend that extra time in class putting together a very neat and creative final draft to present to their classmates. We have never had a problem with students being done with the entire process several days before the due date. However, if you find you do have students with a day or two of extra class time on their hands, there are a few options you can give them for using their remaining class time. We often gave those students the opportunity to use their class time as a study hall to work on other long-term projects or homework assignments. Some students enjoyed using that time to work as a tutor with other students in the class who needed some one-on-one assistance. Another option would be to give those students time to work on free-writing or journal writing. These are just a few suggestions, and you are certainly not limited to them.

The other type of student that turns in work early is the type that turns in rushed, low-quality work. We had a level of high expectations in our classrooms. If a student turned in a final draft that was crumpled, missing part of the requirements, or sloppily written, we simply handed it back and told him or her it was not acceptable. It did not take long for these students to learn that it was better to take the time to do it right the first time than to have to do it twice.

For the students that turned work in late, we would take 10% off of their grade for every day it was late. For example, if a student turned in a rough draft that was worth 50 points one day late, we would grade it according to the rubric breakdown and then take 5 points off. This was a standard rule in our classroom that we enforced consistently.

With the students that simply did not turn in work, we would contact the parents and, if necessary, set up a form of daily communication with them using the assignment books. Those students became responsible for showing us their planners each morning with a parent signature on it. Whenever they completed an assignment during the school day, they were required to bring it and their planners up to us to check off and initial as being completed. Parents were informed that any assignment without our initials was not completed at school and therefore became homework. Any concerns that the parents or we had could easily be noted in the assignment book. This was just another way of keeping the lines of communication open between parents and teacher as well as to inform parents about what their child was doing in school.

RECOMMENDED INSTRUCTION ON OUTLINING, SUMMARIZING, AND USING THE WRITING PROCESS: INCORPORATING SIX TRAIT WRITING

As we mentioned earlier in the book, there are three aspects to our program that we felt helped to make it a success; ASAP Time, our Rubric Assignments, and the time spent outlining a portion of our textbook. Our textbook, *Write Idea* (Macmillan/ McGraw-Hill School Publishing Co., 1993), had sections to it that not only showed the students how to use the writing process to become better writers but also went into detail on how to use the elements of writing to improve on their work.

Outlining the text served many purposes. First of all, we waited until students had experience writing at least two rubric assignments before going into this type of instruction. Once students had a good feel for using the writing process, we were able to refer back to that experience when going over the text and apply the message of the text to their writing experience.

Second, we used this time to teach students how to outline and summarize information. These skills, important in reading comprehension and note-taking strategies, are especially important for students in higher grade levels. We read the text aloud as a class, discussed the meaning of the message, and applied it to the experience the students had had up to that point with their rubric assignments. We then chose students to summarize a section and put it into their own words. We used an overhead to demonstrate the outline format, using the students' paraphrased words, and the students copied the outline into their composition books.

Once we were done with this three-week instruction, we gave the students an open-book test to assess their abilities in reading an outline. This not only reinforced the key elements of good writing but also taught students how to read an outline (which we discovered is a very different skill from writing one).

Finally, this provided the students with instruction on using the writing process and the elements of good writing techniques. The elements we focused on were ones that have always been important for students to learn in developing any good piece of writing. Essentially, we were teaching students Six Trait Writing. The chart below lists the topics we outlined in our text, as well as what trait they fall under.

What we covered from our text	What "trait" it falls under
• Audience awareness and purpose	• Ideas
• Seeing the "big picture"	• Organization
• Leads and endings	• Organization
• Reordering and rearranging	• Organization
• Sentence style and variety	• Fluency
• Building paragraphs	• Fluency
– Topic sentences and details	• Fluency
– Transition words, phrases, and conjunctions	• Fluency
– Dialogue	• Fluency
• Using visual language	• Word Choice
• Clarifying and refining	• Word Choice
• Focusing on elaboration	• Word Choice
• Voice, tone, and mood	• Voice
• Conferencing	• Conventions

As you can see, Six Trait Writing is incorporated into every aspect of our program. We focused on conventions during ASAP Time, each trait as it applied to the students' writing during conference time, and as an

---

How to Incorporate Six Trait Writing

- During ASAP Time
- While conferencing with students on their rough drafts
- As an instructional strategy to teach students how to outline and summarize information

---

instructional strategy to teach students how to outline and summarize information.

This type of instruction could be done all at once (which is the way we chose to do it because we taught thematically), or it could be broken up into a week at a time throughout the year, while you focus your instruction on what you see the students having the most trouble with in their writing assignments.

SETTING UP YOUR GRADE BOOK

The format of the rubrics makes record keeping very easy. Depending on the length of the assignment, you may have anywhere from two to three published pieces of writing in a nine-week grading period. Figure 2.8 is an example of how we set up our grade books to record students' grades.

Figure 2.8

| | Autobiography | | | | | | | Legend | | | | | | | | |
	Pre-write (5)	Rough Draft (50)	Final Draft (40)	Presentation (5)	Total (100)	Grade		Pre-write (5)	Rough Draft (40)	Final Draft (50)	Presentation (5)	Total (100)	Grade		Outline Test (100)	Grade
Sara A.	5	40	35	4	84	B		5	35	45	5	90	A−		93	A−
Joseph B.	5	48	40	5	98	A+		5	38	48	5	96	A		95	A
Natalie C.	4	45	38	5	92	A−		5	40	46	5	96	A		85	B
Jordan F.	4	47	40	4	95	A		5	37	45	5	92	A−		80	B−
Patty G.	4	40	30	4	78	C+		5	35	45	4	89	B+		70	C−

To find your students' average grades for the nine-week period, all you have to do is average the two or three overall grades from each assignment (see Figure 2.9).

Figure 2.9

	Autobiography							Legend												
	5	50	40	5	100			5	40	50	5	100			100					
	Pre-write	Rough Draft	Final Draft	Presentation	Total	Grade		Pre-write	Rough Draft	Final Draft	Presentation	Total	Grade		Outline Test	Grade		Average	Grade	
Sara A.	5	40	35	4	84	B		5	35	45	5	90	A–		93	A–		89	B+	
Joseph B.	5	48	40	5	98	A+		5	38	48	5	96	A		95	A		96	A	
Natalie C.	4	45	38	5	92	A–		5	40	46	5	96	A		85	B		91	A–	
Jordan F.	4	47	40	4	95	A		5	37	45	5	92	A–		80	B–		89	B+	
Patty G.	4	40	30	4	78	C+		5	35	45	4	89	B+		70	C–		79	C+	

3

How to Use This Book

There are eleven different sections with writing rubrics in the latter part of this book, although actually, we are providing you with only ten assignments that could be used throughout the course of one school year. The reason for this is that we strongly recommend the first assignment you give the students be either the autobiography or the biography (not both). These assignments are very similar and provide more detailed and specific requirements than the other rubrics to aid the students in understanding what you expect. We found that many students coming into our classrooms did not have much writing experience. Realizing this, we created these assignments to set them up for success with their first writing assignment.

We found that in fifth grade we had more success with students writing autobiographies than biographies. They did a better job writing about their own lives than they did someone else's. However, we have included the biography assignment to give you the option of which one to use in your classroom. We feel middle school students might have more success with writing biographies than our elementary school students did.

- Teacher instruction for each rubric
- Student examples
- Writing rubric
- Supplementary handouts
- Grading rubrics

Each rubric assignment is set up in four to five different sections to aid you with instruction on how to use them.

TEACHER INSTRUCTION FOR EACH RUBRIC

This section is usually three to four pages of specific instructions on how to use each rubric. Each instruction section includes the following information:

- Suggested timeline
- List of handouts provided for this assignment
- Other materials needed
- Introducing the rubric
- How to evaluate the pre-writing, rough draft, and final draft
- Publishing suggestion
- Modifying the rubric

Suggested Timeline

This provides you with a recommended weekly time frame that demonstrates when you might set the due dates for the different parts of the writing assignment. This is roughly how much time we gave our fifth graders to work on these assignments. Depending on your students' abilities, and taking into consideration holidays or time off, you may need to adjust the time frame to better meet your needs; older students may not need as much time, younger students may need more.

List of Handouts Provided for This Assignment

This section simply lists all the blackline masters that are needed for the assignment. We have provided you with two forms of the rubric. One is if you want to use it as a student contract only; the other requires a parent signature as well. We found it helpful to require a parent signature in elementary school. It was one way we kept parents informed on what their child was doing in school since we were not sending papers home everyday. We required students to return the signature portion within two days; otherwise we would contact their parents.

Other Materials Needed

This section explains what other materials you may need in order for the students to complete the assignment.

Introducing the Rubric

The way to introduce the rubric remains primarily the same for each assignment. You pass out the rubric to the students, read it over together section by section, answering any questions the students may have as you go along. Students need to fill in the due dates for each part of the process on the rubric itself. This would also be the time to have students take out their assignment books and fill in the due dates in their calendars as well. Instruction on how to use the supplementary handouts is also provided in this section. This usually takes an entire class period to go over with the students.

How to Evaluate the Pre-writing, Rough Draft, and Final Draft

These sections explain how we assigned points for each part of the process based on what was required. A detailed explanation on how to evaluate the student's work is provided.

Publishing Suggestion

For the assignments that do not require the students to publish their own writing, we provide you with information on how we published them. Of course, this is not the only way it could be done, but it does provide an idea of where to start.

Modifying the Rubric

This section expands on other ways you might change or use the assignment to meet different needs or topics in your classroom.

STUDENT EXAMPLES

Student examples, when provided, will appear after the teacher instructions and before the writing rubric. These examples are taken from actual work that our fifth graders produced when they were in our classrooms. We did our best to include excerpts from final drafts typed exactly as the students wrote them. That explains why you may find spelling, punctuation, and grammatical errors within the text. Remember, fifth graders wrote these.

WRITING RUBRIC

After the teacher instruction pages, you will find both forms of the actual writing rubric. The rubric itself is usually two pages in length.

SUPPLEMENTARY HANDOUTS

Located behind the rubrics are blackline masters of any supplementary materials required for the assignment. Instruction on how to use these handouts is provided in the teacher instruction segment under the section "Introducing the Rubric," unless otherwise stated. Not all assignments will have supplementary handouts.

GRADING RUBRICS

The last page of each section is a reproducible page with grading rubrics for both the rough draft and the final draft (which also incorporates the presentation grade). These were the grading sheets we sent home with the students after evaluating their work (note: pre-writing grades were written in the students' composition books on the pre-writing page). We usually attached these to the weekly progress reports we sent home to parents. Another option is to staple the Rough Draft Grading Rubric into the student's composition book behind the rough draft. The Final Draft Grading Rubric could also be attached to the final draft when returned to the student. Any comments about the final draft should be placed on this sheet, *not* the student's work. The final draft should not be edited, but simply returned to the students with the grading rubric. Also, when recording the student's presentation grade on the grading rubric, you might want to circle any requirement the student did not fulfill so he or she is aware of what to work on for next time.

PART II

Writing Rubrics and Handouts

4

Autobiography

Suggested Timeline

	Monday	Tuesday	Wednesday	Thursday	Friday
Week 1	Introduce Rubric			Pre-write is due	
Week 2					Rough Draft is due Conferences
Week 3	Conferences			Final Draft is due Presentations	Presentations

Handouts Provided for This Assignment

Autobiography rubric (three pages)

Pre-writing Guide (one page)

Rough draft and final draft/presentation grading rubrics (one page)

Introducing the Rubric

The first day of the three-week project should be spent introducing the rubric. Read it aloud to the class section by section, answering any questions the students may have as you go along. Have students fill in the due dates for each part of the process in the space provided on the rubric. Students should also fill in the due dates for each part of the process in their assignment books.

When going over the pre-writing section of the rubric, be sure to take the time to review the Pre-writing Guide with the students. This breaks down what kind of information should be included in each paragraph of the assignment. Because this is usually the first writing assignment we give the students, we feel it is important to specify the number of paragraphs it should be as well as what to include in each one. This gives the students a strict guide to follow and lets them know exactly what is expected.

How to Evaluate the Pre-writing

The pre-writing is worth 5 points. That breaks down to 1 point for each paragraph that is properly clustered or outlined according to the Pre-writing Guide.

How to Evaluate the Rough Draft

The rough draft for this assignment is probably one of the easiest for the students to produce because of the detailed Pre-writing Guide. We found that many students coming into our classrooms did not have much experience writing complete sentences or paragraphs. In fact, many students had never gone through the entire writing process. Realizing this, we created the Pre-writing Guide to set them up for success with their first writing assignment.

When evaluating the students' rough drafts, points should be assigned as follows:

a. *Five paragraphs in length* (5 points): 1 point for each paragraph.

b. *At least four sentences per paragraph* (5 points): 1 point for each paragraph that is written using at least four sentences.

c. *Followed the Pre-writing Guide* (10 points): 2 points for each paragraph that includes all the information stated in the Pre-writing Guide.

d. *Made sense and was told in a logical order* (10 points): think percentagewise when assigning these points. On a scale of 1 to 10, how well did the rough draft make sense, and was it told in a logical order?

e. *Followed Composition Book Guidelines* (20 points): 2 points for following each guideline.

How to Evaluate the Final Draft

When evaluating the students' final drafts, points should be assigned as follows:

a. *Used correct spelling, punctuation, and grammar* (10 points): spelling (3 points), punctuation (4 points), and grammar (3 points).

b. *Corrections from conference were made* (10 points): on a scale of 1 to 10, how well did the student make the revisions discussed during your conference?

c. *Followed the correct format* (10 points): on a scale of 1 to 10, how well did the student maintain the format stated in the Pre-writing Guide?

d. *Neatness and care were taken in publication* (10 points): on a scale of 1 to 10, was the final copy neat, easy to read, and typed or written in cursive (in black or blue ink only)?

Publishing Suggestion

We collected all the final drafts and bound them into one class book. You could have a student design the cover, or design the cover yourself. We simply used our school's binding machine. The book was always available for our students to read in class. We also had it accessible for parents to enjoy while waiting for a conference or during Open House.

Modifying the Rubric

If you have older students with more writing experience, you may not need to provide such a detailed assignment. Instead of giving students the Pre-writing Guide, you might just brainstorm as a class what to include in the assignment.

Also, instead of publishing these in a class book, you might require students to publish their own autobiographies in book form with actual pictures or illustrations on each page. Just remember that anything you require the students to do must be stated in the rubric. Therefore, the points and requirements would have to be adjusted.

STUDENT EXAMPLES

Excerpts From Several Students' Autobiography Final Drafts

John Perea's first paragraph

As a person, I have always had a strange personality. I like certain things such as Lego's, music, math, and Dinosaurs. My favorite foods are Mexican, Italian, and Chinese. My family must have been big because I am part Hispanic, Irish, German, and Basque. I was born on May 29, 1990 in Albuquerque, New Mexico.

Samantha Phelps's second paragraph

I love traveling to different states. Just the soft rumble of the van as it rolls ever closer to its destination makes me feel so relaxed and comfortable. My family and I have been to Utah, Arizona and Colorado loads of times. . . . But, as much as I love traveling, it's always good to be home. Though, some time in my life, I would like to go to Disney Land, Washington D.C., and maybe even visit Carlsbad Caverns again.

Evelynn Moore's third paragraph

I enjoy singing because I think I have a wonderful voice but my family doesn't think I do. I also enjoy dancing, playing instruments, exploring, school, and I love to use my imagination. . . . My imagination is quite big because I love to think. I love to read because it is fun. I love school because I love learning new things.

Holly Twitchell's fourth paragraph

In my spare time I love working on crafts, and following directions. During the summer time I play tennis with my mom. If I'm in my room, sometimes I'll talk to my frogs. They help me figure out my problems. I have 2 frogs, one's pink but she doesn't have a name, and the other's name is Froggy, he's green and his legs are crossed. They are very helpful to me.

Laura Perea's fifth paragraph

There are many things that people don't know about me. For instance, I am allergic to Penicillan and cephalexin. Last year, my brother and I were picking peaches from our peach trees when I found out that I was allergic to the peach fuzz! Two of the things I hate most are peanut butter and mustard. My favorite food is spaghetti. I eat it at least twice a week. I love to speak Spanish, but I still have much to learn. Maybe next year I can take a Spanish class. Writing this paper really helped me learn more about myself.

Figure 4.1 Laura Perea's Pre-write

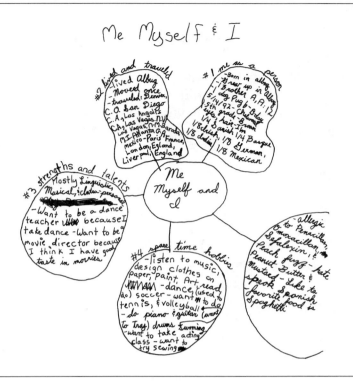

Figure 4.2 A Page From Laura Perea's Rough Draft

balloon company. My dad works
at the University of New Mexico,
~~and he works~~ with computers. ~~And~~
I have one dog called a chinese
pug, and her ~~own~~ name is
Rosy Daffodil Perea. I have
~~brown~~ brown eyes, brown hair,
and slightly dark skin. I ~~am~~
am 1/4 Spanish, 1/4 Basque, 1/8
Irish, 1/8 German, 1/8 Indian ~~1/8~~
and 1/8 Mexican.

~~I have~~ all my life

Name: _____

AUTOBIOGRAPHY RUBRIC

For your first writing assignment, you will be responsible for writing an autobiography. Your final draft will be presented to the class and published in a class book. The following steps must be completed for this writing assignment:

1. <u>Pre-write</u>: (Worth 5 points: _____)

   Due: _____

You will be provided with a Pre-writing Guide to help give you ideas about how to organize your paper.

2. <u>Rough Draft</u>: (Worth 50 points: _____)

   Due: _____

Your rough draft will be graded as follows:

   a. Five paragraphs in length (5 points)
   b. At least four sentences per paragraph (5 points)
   c. Followed the Pre-writing Guide (10 points)
   d. Made sense and was told in a logical order (10 points)
   e. Followed Composition Book Guidelines (20 points)

3. <u>Conference</u>:

Before you begin work on your final draft, you and I must conference about your rough draft. We will discuss all the skills you used well along with skills that need improvement. We will both keep track of these skills to help measure your improvement in writing.

4. <u>Final Draft</u>: (Worth 40 points: _____)
   Due: _____

Your final draft will be graded as follows:

   a. Used correct spelling, punctuation, and grammar (10 points)
   b. Corrections from conference were made (10 points)
   c. Followed the correct format (10 points)
   d. Neatness and care were taken in publication (10 points) (typed or written in cursive—in black or blue ink only)

5. <u>Presentation</u>: (Worth 5 points: _____)

When presenting your autobiography to the class, you will be graded on the following:

   a. Eye contact: did you look at the audience? (1 point)
   b. Volume: could the audience hear you? (1 point)
   c. Clarity: could the audience understand you? (1 point)
   d. Posture: were you standing straight and tall? (1 point)
   e. Pride: did you sound proud of your work? (1 point)

Please cut and return the bottom portion to your teacher. Keep the top portion in your writing folder.

Autobiography Writing Rubric

Student Contract

I understand the writing assignment for which I am responsible. I will turn in my work by the required due dates, being careful to include all mandatory components of this assignment. I understand that anything not completed in class will become homework.

Student signature: _____ Date: _____

5. <u>Presentation</u>: (Worth 5 points: _____)

When presenting your autobiography to the class, you will be graded on the following:

  a. Eye contact: did you look at the audience? (1 point)
  b. Volume: could the audience hear you? (1 point)
  c. Clarity: could the audience understand you? (1 point)
  d. Posture: were you standing straight and tall? (1 point)
  e. Pride: did you sound proud of your work? (1 point)

Please cut and return the bottom portion to your teacher. Keep the top portion in your writing folder.

Autobiography Writing Rubric

Student Contract With Parent Signature

I understand the writing assignment for which I am responsible. I will turn in my work by the required due dates, being careful to include all mandatory components of this assignment. I understand that anything not completed in class will become homework.

Student signature: _____   Date: _____

I am aware of the writing assignment for which my child is responsible as well as the due dates for each part. I understand that anything not completed in class will become homework.

Parent signature: _____   Date: _____

Name: _____

AUTOBIOGRAPHY PRE-WRITING GUIDE

An autobiography is the story of your life written by you. You will be writing your own autobiography in paragraph form and in complete sentences. Use the following outline to guide you in your writing.

First paragraph:

    This should include information about who you are as a person, as well as information about your family and background.

Second paragraph:

    This should include information about where you have lived and where you have traveled. If you have not traveled much, you might want to include where you would like to travel someday.

Third paragraph:

    This should include information about your academic strengths and talents. Also include information on what you would like to be when you grow up and why you feel you would be good at it.

Fourth paragraph:

    This should include information about what you like to do in your spare time. Write about your hobbies, sports interests, musical talents, etc. Also include any information about hobbies or interests you would like to try in the future.

Fifth paragraph:

    This should include information about yourself that you haven't already mentioned and that no one else in the class knows. It could be as simple as saying that you like peanut butter and banana sandwiches, sharing something about things you are allergic to, or it could be as personal as sharing that you had your tonsils taken out this summer. Whatever it is, make sure it is something that you are willing to share with the whole class.

Name: _____

AUTOBIOGRAPHY ROUGH DRAFT GRADING RUBRIC

Five paragraphs in length..worth 5 points: _____

At least four sentences per paragraph ....worth 5 points: _____

Followed the Pre-writing Guide ....worth 10 points: _____

Made sense and was told in a logical order..................worth 10 points: _____

Followed Composition Book Guidelines........................worth 20 points: _____

Worth 50 points: _____

Percentage/Letter Grade: _____

Name: _____

AUTOBIOGRAPHY FINAL DRAFT
AND PRESENTATION GRADING RUBRIC

Used correct spelling, punctuation, and grammar ....worth 10 points: ____

Corrections from conference were made ....worth 10 points: ____

Followed the correct format...worth 10 points: ____

Neatness and care were taken in publication ....worth 10 points: ____

Presentation:
eye contact, volume, clarity, posture, pride ....worth 5 points: ____

Worth 45 points: ____

Percentage/Letter Grade: ____

5

Biography

TEACHER INSTRUCTION FOR BIOGRAPHY RUBRIC

Suggested Timeline

	Monday	Tuesday	Wednesday	Thursday	Friday
Week 1	Introduce Rubric			Pre-write is due	
Week 2					Rough Draft is due Conferences
Week 3	Conferences			Final Draft and Venn Diagram are due Presentations	Presentations

Handouts Provided for This Assignment

Biography rubric (three pages)

Pre-writing Guide (one page)

Venn diagram example (one page)

Rough draft and final draft/presentation grading rubrics (one page)

Introducing the Rubric

The first day of the three-week project should be spent introducing the rubric. Read it aloud to the class section by section, answering any questions the students may have as you go along. Have students fill in the due dates for each part of the process in the space provided on the rubric. Students should also fill in the due dates for each part of the process in their assignment books.

When going over the pre-writing section of the rubric, be sure to take the time to review the Pre-writing Guide with the students. This breaks down what kind of information should be included in each paragraph of the assignment. Because this is usually the first writing assignment we give the students, we feel it is important to specify the number of paragraphs it should be as well as what to include in each one. This gives the students a strict guide to follow and lets them know exactly what is expected.

How to Evaluate the Pre-writing

The pre-writing is worth 5 points. That breaks down to 1 point for each paragraph that is properly clustered or outlined according to the Pre-writing Guide.

How to Evaluate the Rough Draft

The rough draft for this assignment is probably one of the easiest for the students to produce because of the detailed Pre-writing Guide. We found that many students coming into our classrooms did not have much experience writing complete sentences or paragraphs. In fact, many students had never gone through the entire writing process. Realizing this, we created the Pre-writing Guide to set them up for success with their first writing assignment.

When evaluating the students' rough drafts, points should be assigned as follows:

a. *Five paragraphs in length* (5 points): 1 point for each paragraph.

b. *At least four sentences per paragraph* (5 points): 1 point for each paragraph that is written using at least four sentences.

c. *Followed the Pre-writing Guide* (5 points): 1 point for each paragraph that includes all the information stated in the Pre-writing Guide.

d. *Made sense and was told in a logical order* (5 points): on a scale of 1 to 5, how well did the rough draft make sense, and was it told in a logical order?

e. *Followed Composition Book Guidelines* (20 points): 2 points for following each guideline.

How to Evaluate the Final Draft

When evaluating the students' final drafts, points should be assigned as follows:

a. *Used correct spelling, punctuation, and grammar* (10 points): spelling (3 points), punctuation (4 points), and grammar (3 points).

b. *Corrections from conference were made* (10 points): on a scale of 1 to 10, how well did the student make the revisions discussed during your conference?

c. *Followed the rough draft format* (10 points): on a scale of 1 to 10, how well did the student maintain the format stated in the Pre-writing Guide?

d. *Neatness and care were taken in publication* (10 points): on a scale of 1 to 10, was the final copy neat, easy to read, and typed or written in cursive (in black or blue ink only)?

Publishing Suggestion

We collected all the final drafts and bound them into one class book. You could have a student design the cover, or design the cover yourself. We simply used our school's binding machine. The book was always available for our students to read in class. We also had it accessible for parents to enjoy while waiting for a conference or during Open House.

Modifying the Rubric

If you have older students with more writing experience, you may not need to provide such a detailed assignment. Instead of giving students the Pre-writing Guide, have them generate their own interview questions after discussing as a class possible interview topics. Also, you may want to change the assignment to state how many words or pages are required instead of how many paragraphs or sentences it should include. Just remember, anything you require the students to do must be stated in the rubric. Therefore, the points and requirements would have to be adjusted.

Name: _____

BIOGRAPHY RUBRIC

For your first writing assignment, you will be responsible for conducting an interview with a classmate and writing a biography on that person. Your final draft will be presented to the class and published in a class book. You and your partner will also be responsible for introducing each other to the rest of the class with the visual aid of a Venn diagram. The following steps must be completed for this writing assignment:

1. <u>Pre-write</u>: (Worth 5 points: _____)

    Due: _____

This will take place in the form of interview questions and answers. You will be provided with a Pre-writing Guide to give you ideas about how to organize your paper, as well as sample questions you might ask your partner. You are not limited to these ideas. Please feel free to add to them.

2. <u>Rough Draft</u>: (Worth 40 points: _____)

    Due: _____

Your rough draft will be graded as follows:

   a. Five paragraphs in length (5 points)
   b. At least four sentences per paragraph (5 points)
   c. Followed the Pre-writing Guide (5 points)
   d. Made sense and was told in a logical order (5 points)
   e. Followed Composition Book Guidelines (20 points)

3. <u>Conference</u>:

Before you begin work on your final draft, you and I must conference about your rough draft. We will discuss all the skills you used well along with skills that need improvement. We will both keep track of these skills to help measure your improvement in writing.

4. <u>Final Draft</u>: (Worth 40 points: _____)

    Due: _____

Your final draft will be graded as follows:

   a. Used correct spelling, punctuation, and grammar (10 points)

b. Corrections from conference were made (10 points)
c. Followed the correct format (10 points)
d. Neatness and care were taken in publication (10 points) (typed or written in cursive—in black or blue ink only)

5. <u>Venn Diagram</u>: (Worth 10 points: _____)

Due: _____

When presenting your Venn diagram to the class, the following guidelines must be met:

a. Large enough for the whole class to see (2 points)
b. Neat in appearance (2 points)
c. Creative; illustrations were included for visual appeal (3 points)
d. Diagram was used properly (3 points)

6. <u>Presentation</u>: (Worth 5 points: _____)

When presenting your biography to the class, you will be graded on the following:

a. Eye contact: did you look at the audience? (1 point)
b. Volume: could the audience hear you? (1 point)
c. Clarity: could the audience understand you? (1 point)
d. Posture: were you standing straight and tall? (1 point)
e. Pride: did you sound proud of your work? (1 point)

Please cut and return the bottom portion to your teacher. Keep the top portion in your writing folder.

Biography Writing Rubric

Student Contract

I understand the writing assignment for which I am responsible. I will turn in my work by the required due dates, being careful to include all mandatory components of this assignment. I understand that anything not completed in class will become homework.

Student signature: _____ Date: _____

    b. Corrections from conference were made (10 points)
    c. Followed the correct format (10 points)
    d. Neatness and care were taken in publication (10 points) (typed or written in cursive - in black or blue ink only)

5. <u>Venn Diagram</u>: (Worth 10 points: _____)

   Due: _____

When presenting your Venn diagram to the class, the following guidelines must be met:

    a. Large enough for the whole class to see (2 points)
    b. Neat in appearance (2 points)
    c. Creative; illustrations were included for visual appeal (3 points)
    d. Diagram was used properly (3 points)

6. <u>Presentation</u>: (Worth 5 points: _____)

When presenting your biography to the class, you will be graded on the following:

    a. Eye contact: did you look at the audience? (1 point)
    b. Volume: could the audience hear you? (1 point)
    c. Clarity: could the audience understand you? (1 point)
    d. Posture: were you standing straight and tall? (1 point)
    e. Pride: did you sound proud of your work? (1 point)

Please cut and return the bottom portion to your teacher. Keep the top portion in your writing folder.

Biography Writing Rubric

Student Contract With Parent Signature

I understand the writing assignment for which I am responsible. I will turn in my work by the required due dates, being careful to include all mandatory components of this assignment. I understand that anything not completed in class will become homework.

Student signature: _____ Date: _____

I am aware of the writing assignment for which my child is responsible as well as the due dates for each part. I understand that anything not completed in class will become homework.

Parent signature: _____ Date: _____

Name: _____

BIOGRAPHY PRE-WRITING GUIDE

A biography is the story of someone's life written by someone else. You will be writing a biography about another person in this class. You must write it in paragraph form and in complete sentences. Use the following outline to guide you in your writing.

First paragraph:
>   What is your name?
>   When and where were you born?
>   How old are you?
>   Who are your parents?
>   Do you have any brothers or sisters? (what are their names and ages?)
>   What else should we know about your family?

Second paragraph:
>   Where do you live?
>   Where else have you lived?
>   Where have you traveled?
>   Where would you like to travel (or even live)?

Third paragraph:
>   What are your academic strengths and talents?
>   What do you want to be when you grow up?
>   Why do you want to be that?
>   Why would you be good at it?

Fourth paragraph:
>   What are your hobbies (what do you like to do in your spare time)?
>   Is there anything that you absolutely dislike to do? If so, what?

Fifth paragraph:
>   For this paragraph, you will be required to make up your own interview questions:

>   1. _____
>   2. _____

WHAT IS A VENN DIAGRAM?

The Venn diagram below is a graphic organizer that demonstrates the relationship between two students. It also shows their similarities and differences.

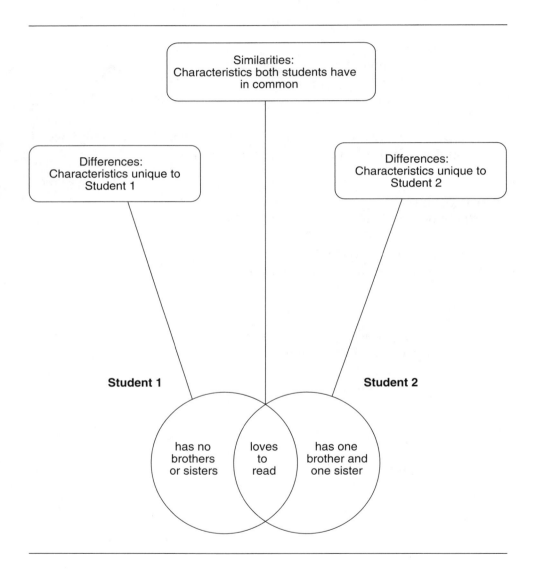

Name: _____

BIOGRAPHY ROUGH DRAFT GRADING RUBRIC

Five paragraphs in length.................................... worth 5 points: _____

At least four sentences per paragraph .... worth 5 points: _____

Followed the Pre-writing Guide............................ worth 5 points: _____

Made sense and was told in a logical order .... worth 5 points: _____

Followed Composition Book Guidelines................ worth 20 points: _____

Worth 40 points: _____

Percentage/Letter Grade: _____

Name: _____

BIOGRAPHY FINAL DRAFT AND
PRESENTATION GRADING RUBRIC

Used correct spelling, punctuation, and grammar... worth 10 points: ____

Corrections from conference were made................. worth 10 points: ____

Followed the correct format.................................. worth 10 points: ____

Neatness and care were taken in publication.......... worth 10 points: ____

Presentation:
eye contact, volume, clarity, posture, pride............ worth 5 points: ____

Worth 45 points: ____

Percentage/Letter Grade: ____

6

Persuasive Essay

TEACHER INSTRUCTION FOR ESSAY RUBRIC

Suggested Timeline

	Monday	Tuesday	Wednesday	Thursday	Friday
Week 1	Introduce Rubric *Mini-lesson			Pre-write is due	
Week 2					Rough Draft is due Conferences
Week 3	Conferences				Final Draft is due Presentations

*Essay format, topic sentences, and supporting details.

Handouts Provided for This Assignment

Essay rubric (three pages)

Essay pre-writing examples (two pages)

Essay example (one page)

Rough draft and final draft/presentation grading rubrics (one page)

Introducing the Rubric

The first day of the three-week project should be spent introducing the rubric. Read it aloud to the class section by section, answering any questions the students may have as you go along. Have students fill in the due dates for each part of the process in the space provided on the rubric. Students should also fill in the due dates for each part of the process in their assignment book calendars.

When going over the rough draft section of the rubric, be sure to take the time to review the essay format with the students (page two of the rubric). If there is enough time, pass out the pre-writing and essay examples to the students (otherwise, do it the following day). Go over these together, focusing your instruction on topic sentences and supporting details. Emphasize that part of their grades will be based on whether or not they have a topic sentence and three supporting examples in each paragraph. When reading the sample essay, it is also helpful to have students underline these in each paragraph. In doing this, it becomes much easier for the students to see the connection between the pre-writing and the actual essay, as well as how to use topic sentences and supporting details.

How to Evaluate the Pre-writing

The pre-writing is worth 5 points. That breaks down to 1 point for each paragraph that is properly clustered or outlined according to the essay format.

How to Evaluate the Rough Draft

Points should be assigned as follows:

a. *Written in five-paragraph essay format* (25 points):
   - Five paragraphs (5 points): 1 point for each paragraph.
   - Topic sentences (5 points): 1 point for each topic sentence.
   - Supporting examples (10 points): since there should be at least nine supporting examples (three for each reason), that is approximately 1 point per example.
   - Organization (5 points): on a scale of 1 to 5, how well did the student organize the essay? Did the rough draft follow the organization detailed in the pre-writing?

b. *Followed Composition Book Guidelines* (10 points): 1 point for following each guideline.

c. *Persuasive and convincing* (10 points): on a scale of 1 to 10, how persuasive and convincing was the essay?

d. *Contained at least 300 words* (5 points): deduct 1 point for every ten words below 300.

How to Evaluate the Final Draft

When evaluating the students' final drafts, points should be assigned as follows:

a. *Used correct spelling, punctuation, and grammar* (10 points): spelling (3 points), punctuation (4 points), and grammar (3 points).

b. *Corrections from conference were made* (10 points): on a scale of 1 to 10, how well did the student make the revisions discussed during your conference?

c. *Written in five-paragraph essay format with at least 300 words* (10 points): five paragraphs (3 points), topic sentences (3 points), supporting details (2 points), and at least 300 words (2 points).

d. *Neatness and care were taken in publication* (10 points): on a scale of 1 to 10, was the final copy neat, easy to read, and typed or written in cursive (in black or blue ink only)?

Publishing Suggestion

We collected all the final drafts and bound them into one class book. You could have a student design the cover or design the cover yourself. We simply used our school's binding machine. The book was always available for our students to read in class. We also had it accessible for parents to enjoy while waiting for a conference or during our school's Literacy Fair.

Modifying the Rubric

This assignment can be used with any essay topic. The format for the essay always stays the same. We found that students had an easier time understanding how to write an essay when they were writing about something they had personal experience with and enjoyed doing. This made it easier for students to come up with the details to support their topic sentences. Even our low-ability students could usually write a good-quality essay when given this assignment. Once the students learned the format, they could easily write an essay on any given topic. It is important to remember that anything you require the students to do must be stated in the rubric. Therefore, the points and requirements would have to be adjusted.

STUDENT EXAMPLES

Excerpts From Laura Perea's Persuasive Essay

Figure 6.1   Pre-write

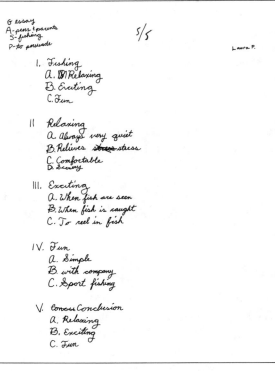

Figure 6.2   Rough Draft

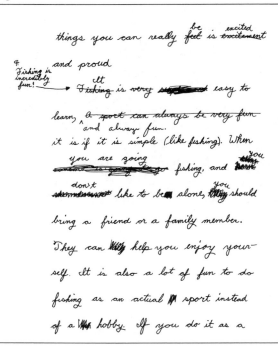

Excerpts From Several Students' Final Drafts

Final Draft	**Fishing**

By Laura Perea

Fishing is something that just about anyone can, and should do. It takes a lot of patience. There are plenty of reasons why someone should try fishing. Some of the main reasons are because it's relaxing, exciting, and it's really fun. It is very challenging to think of a reason why somebody wouldn't like fishing.

Fishing can actually relieve stress. It gives people time to daydream. It also gives people time to themselves. The scenery of the lake is always so quiet and beautiful. Just to sit in front of the water with nothing to bother you whatsoever is so comfortable and relaxing.

Fishing can also be very exciting. Especially whenever fish are seen. That tells you that the fish are ready to grab your hook. The best part about fishing is catching a fish. Then you can reel it in. Once you actually have it out of the water, the only two things you can really feel is excited and proud.

Fishing is incredibly fun! It is easy to learn, and always fun. When you are going fishing, and you don't like to be alone, you should bring a friend or a family member along. They can help you enjoy yourself. It is also a lot of fun to do fishing as an actual sport instead of a hobby. If you do it as a sport, you can go to different competitions and see who can catch the best fish.

As you can probably see, fishing is a great hobby. I hope that someday you will try fishing. It is relaxing, and exciting. Best of all, it's fun!

Bored? What's That!

By John Perea

Have you ever been stumped with nothing to do on a rainy day? I have something you should try; they are called Lego's. You may have heard of them before. Lego's are fun! The pieces are neat and can fit <u>any</u> topic. Lego's can <u>exercise your imagination</u>! The pieces are all different so it's easy to think up new things. Lego's are <u>challenging</u>! You have to fit the pieces just right in order to make a model work.

Playing an Instrument

By Kiley Kartchner

Instruments are also educational. They are educational because you learn a new language. Not the kind where you use words, but the kind where you read notes and play them. It's easy to learn. Music is also educational because you learn where your fingers go. Fingers are used to hold an instrument, some push down string, buttons, and keys, and some pluck! It's educational by treating the instrument carefully. If you don't treat it carefully it could go out of tune, break, get dirty and more.

Piano

By Samantha Phelps

Another reason to try piano is that it will make you feel good knowing you can play a unique instrument. People will invite you to parties and ask you to play for them, and there's no better feeling than telling people you can play Mozart or Bach's music on the piano. You will also feel good knowing how to read music, which will come in handy if you ever become a music teacher. Everyone will admire your unique talent. Now that's something to feel good about!

B'Ball

By Victor Ramos

One of the best reasons to try basketball is that it teaches kids and adults how to learn teamwork, and cooperation. You have to learn to play with other kids and adults on your team. You also have to learn to cooperate with players on your team. Basketball is a team sport and to win games the whole team has to do good not just one player. It is also a great way for young kids to get along with each other.

Biking

By Molly Espinoza

Finally, one last great reason is that bikes are not like cars or like trucks and do not require any gas at all. So, it saves the little gas we have on earth and it does not pollute the air. Also you will not be cooped up in your car. So when you ride a bike, you not only help yourself but everyone else around you as well so you and everyone else around you can breathe better air.

So as you can see a bike is a very good and interesting invention. It is great exercise, and it doesn't require any gas. All these reasons go into one little machine. So give it a whirl. Oh! And do not forget to wear your helmet!

Name: _____

PERSUASIVE ESSAY RUBRIC

For the next three weeks you will be working on writing a persuasive essay. You must convince me, in 300 words or more, that your favorite hobby is something that I should try. You will be graded as follows:

1. <u>Pre-write</u>: (Worth 5 points: _____)

   Due: _____

Your pre-writing should include what your topic is, the three reasons you think I should try it, and the specific examples you are going to use to support your reasons. This may be done in either outline form or cluster form.

2. <u>Rough Draft</u>: (Worth 50 points: _____)

   Due: _____

Your rough draft will be graded as follows:
   a. Written in five paragraph essay format (see attached sheet - 25 points)
   b. Followed Composition Book Guidelines (10 points)
   c. Persuasive and convincing (10 points)
   d. Contained at least 300 words (5 points)

3. <u>Conference</u>:

Before you begin work on your final draft, you and I must conference about your rough draft. We will discuss all the skills you used well along with skills that need improvement. We will both keep track of these skills to help measure your improvement in writing.

4. <u>Final Draft</u>: (Worth 40 points: _____)

   Due: _____

Your final draft will be graded as follows:
   a. Used correct spelling, punctuation, and grammar (10 points)
   b. Corrections from conference were made (10 points)
   c. Written in 5-paragraph essay format with at least 300 words (10 points)
   d. Neatness and care were taken in publication (10 points)

5. <u>Presentation</u>: (Worth 5 points: _____)

When presenting your essay to the class, you will be graded on your eye contact, volume, clarity, posture, and pride (one point for each).

ESSAY FORMAT

I. Introduction: State your topic
   A. Give reason #1
   B. Give reason #2
   C. Give reason #3

II. State your first reason
   A. Back it up with a specific example
   B. Back it up with a second specific example
   C. Back it up with a third specific example

III. State your second reason
   A. Back it up with a specific example
   B. Back it up with a second specific example
   C. Back it up with a third specific example

IV. State your third reason
   A. Back it up with a specific example
   B. Back it up with a second specific example
   C. Back it up with a third specific example

V. Conclusion: Restate your topic
   A. Give reason #1
   B. Give reason #2
   C. Give reason #3

Please cut and return the bottom portion to your teacher. Keep the top portion in your writing folder.

Essay Writing Rubric

Student Contract

I understand the writing assignment for which I am responsible. I will turn in my work by the required due dates, being careful to include all mandatory components of this assignment. I understand that anything not completed in class will become homework.

Student signature: _____   Date: _____

ESSAY FORMAT

I. Introduction: State your topic
 A. Give reason #1
 B. Give reason #2
 C. Give reason #3

II. State your first reason
 A. Back it up with a specific example
 B. Back it up with a second specific example
 C. Back it up with a third specific example

III. State your second reason
 A. Back it up with a specific example
 B. Back it up with a second specific example
 C. Back it up with a third specific example

IV. State your third reason
 A. Back it up with a specific example
 B. Back it up with a second specific example
 C. Back it up with a third specific example

V. Conclusion: Restate your topic
 A. Give reason #1
 B. Give reason #2
 C. Give reason #3

Please cut and return the bottom portion to your teacher. Keep the top portion in your writing folder.

Essay Writing Rubric

Student Contract With Parent Signature

I understand the writing assignment for which I am responsible. I will turn in my work by the required due dates, being careful to include all mandatory components of this assignment. I understand that anything not completed in class will become homework.

Student signature: _____ Date: _____

I am aware of the writing assignment for which my child is responsible as well as the due dates for each part. I understand that anything not completed in class will become homework.

Parent signature: _____ Date: _____

PERSUASIVE ESSAY SAMPLE PRE-WRITE: OUTLINE FORM

G - Essay
A - Peers and parents
S - Country Western dancing
P - To persuade

  I. Country Western dancing
      A. Easy to learn
      B. Great source of exercise
      C. Fun!

 II. Easy to learn
      A. Places offer free lessons
      B. So simple, a child could learn
      C. Basic steps are repeated

III. Great source of exercise
      A. Similar to walking or jogging
      B. Increases endurance and heart rate
      C. Builds muscle tone

 IV. Fun!
      A. Possibilities of moves are endless
          1. Dips
          2. Flips
          3. Drops
          4. Ducks
      B. Listen to good music and move to the beat
      C. Crowd reaction is energizing

  V. Country Western dancing
      A. Easy to learn
      B. Great source of exercise
      C. Fun!

PERSUASIVE ESSAY SAMPLE PRE-WRITE: CLUSTER FORM

Date

G - Essay
A - Peers and adults
S - Country Western dancing
P - To persuade

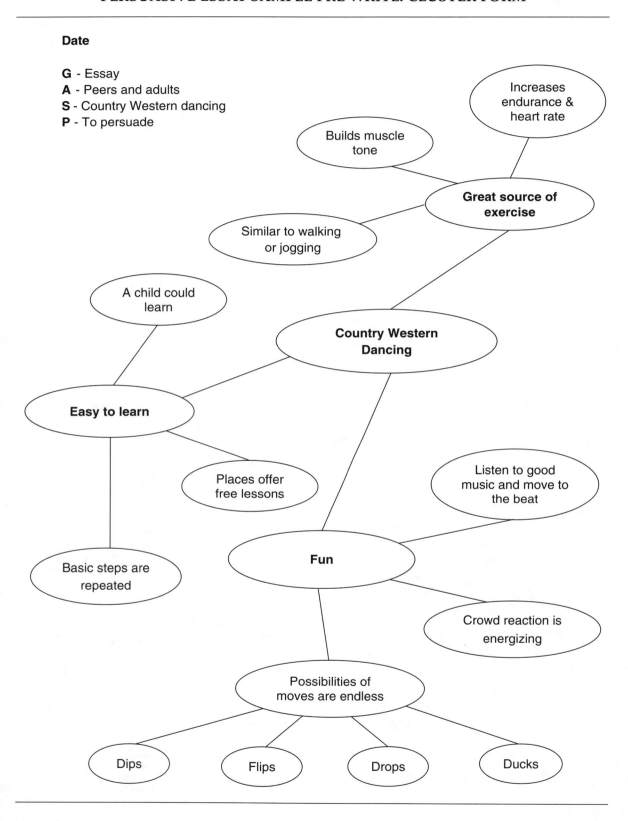

PERSUASIVE ESSAY EXAMPLE

Country Western dancing is an activity that everyone should try. Once you get started, it is something that you will never want to give up. There are many good reasons to try this kind of dancing. However, the most convincing reasons are because it is easy to learn, it is a great source of exercise, and it is a lot of fun to do.

First of all, if you do not know how to dance, it is not a problem. Country Western dancing is very easy to learn. There are several places in town that offer free dance lessons on how to two-step, swing, polka, or waltz. The basic dance steps to these dances are easy enough that even a child could learn them. You will also find that the basic steps are repeated, so there is not a lot of fancy footwork to memorize.

Another good reason to try Country Western dancing is because it is a great source of exercise. When you are dancing, you are doing about the same extent of exercise as walking or jogging, depending on the type of dance. In the waltz or two-step, you are constantly moving at a steady pace. In these two types of dances, like in walking, you are building up your endurance and increasing your heart rate. If you are dancing a swing or a polka, like in jogging, you are moving at a quicker rate; so you are not only increasing your endurance and heart rate, but you are also building on the muscle tone in your arms and legs.

The best reason to try Country Western dancing is because it is so much fun. Once you learn the basic steps, the possibilities of ways you can combine them are endless. Once you get the hang of it, you might even want to try learning some of the more complicated moves, like dips, flips, drops, and ducks. The enjoyment you can get from listening to the music, and moving to the beat of a song in this way is simply indescribable. Although, the most fun is having people in the crowd stop what they are doing just to watch you dance. Sometimes they even applaud. That kind of crowd reaction is energizing, and it is part of what makes Country Western dancing so exciting!

As you can see, there are many good reasons to try Country Western dancing. It is easy to learn, it is a great source of exercise, plus it is lots of fun. So, what is keeping you from trying it? Put on your dancing boots, and get yourself to the nearest dance place for some free lessons on Country Western dancing. See you on the dance floor!

Name: _____

PERSUASIVE ESSAY ROUGH DRAFT GRADING RUBRIC

Written in five-paragraph essay format...................... worth 25 points: _____

    Five paragraphs (5 points)

    Topic sentences (5 points)

    Supporting examples (10 points)

    Organization (5 points)

Followed Composition Book Guidelines .... worth 10 points: _____

Persuasive and convincing....................................... worth 10 points: _____

Contained at least 300 words................................... worth 5 points: _____

Worth 50 points: _____

Percentage/Letter Grade: _____

Name: _____

PERSUASIVE ESSAY FINAL DRAFT
AND PRESENTATION GRADING RUBRIC

Used correct spelling, punctuation, and grammar....... worth 10 points: _____

Corrections from conference were made .... worth 10 points: _____

Written in five paragraph essay format...................... worth 10 points: _____

Neatness and care were taken in publication.............. worth 10 points: _____

Presentation:
eye contact, volume, clarity, posture,
and pride .... worth 5 points: _____

Worth 45 points: _____

Percentage/Letter Grade: _____

7

Research Paper

TEACHER INSTRUCTION FOR RESEARCH PAPER RUBRIC

Suggested Timeline

	Monday	Tuesday	Wednesday	Thursday	Friday
Week 1	Introduce Rubric Pick topics	Trip to the library Mini-lesson: Research Skills	Mini-lesson: Bibliography Card Format and Bibliography Page	Mini-lesson: Note Card Format and Plagiarism	Bibliography Cards are due (end of class)
Week 2					Note Cards are due (end of class)
Week 3	Mini-lesson: Outline Format (using note cards)				Outline is due Mini-lesson: Citing Quotes
Week 4	Mini-lesson: Using the Outline and Note Cards for the Rough Draft				Rough Draft is due Conferences
Week 5	Conferences			Final Draft is due Presentations	Presentations

Handouts Provided for This Assignment

Research paper rubric (four pages)

List of possible topics (one page)

Format for bibliography cards (one page)

Sample bibliography page (one page)

Format for note cards (one page)

Outline example (one page)

Rough draft and final draft/presentation grading rubrics (one page)

Introducing the Rubric

The first day of the five-week project should be spent introducing the rubric. Read it aloud to the class section by section, answering any questions the students may have as you go along. Have students fill in the due dates for each part of the process in the spaces provided on the rubric. Students should also fill in the due dates for each part of the process in their assignment books as well.

Once you have introduced the rubric, take some time to have students *pick topics* for their research. We have included a list of possible topics with the reproducible pages that you could use as an overhead. This list is simply a suggestion. Plenty of information was readily available on each of these topics for the students to use in their research. If a student was interested in researching a topic not on the list, we would certainly give the student that option as long as he or she could find enough information on the topic to fulfill the requirements of the report. Another option would be to brainstorm a list of topics with the class.

A strategy we found both helpful and fair for situations like this was to have students' names on craft sticks placed in a cup. The person whose name was drawn first got first choice from the list of topics, whereas the student whose name was drawn last received the last choice. We tried to provide more topics than there were students so that even the last student had a choice. There was never a question on fairness when we did this.

We also required that each student in the class research a different topic. We did this for two reasons. First of all, there were limited resources available on each topic. Having students research different topics provided them with more information available from our school and public libraries. Second, we wanted to expose the students to a variety of subject matter during their final draft presentations. Requiring this prevented them from having to listen to three or four reports on the same subject.

We implemented this research project during a thematic unit on the study of whales. Because of that, we did not have whales listed as a possible topic choice. However, there was plenty of information available on different types of whales if a student was interested in narrowing that topic to a more manageable one. That could also provide you with several more topics for students to research (beluga whale, blue whale, narwhal, orca whale, sperm whale, etc.).

During the first week of this assignment we would make two *trips to the library*, one to our school library and one to the public library. We coordinated with our school librarian to go over *research skills* with the students during our library time for that week. We would then take students on a field trip to our neighboring public library to find more research materials. If you teach middle school, a field trip to the public library would probably be out of the question. Because of this, we recommend that you take the students to the school library to go over research skills, and allow them to each check out one resource on the topic of their choice. This would eliminate the problem of all resources being checked out to one person. It would also be important to direct students to visit the public library to gather more research materials on their own. Another option would be to check out all your school library materials (on the topics listed) for students to use in the classroom. In doing this, students in different classes would be able to use the same resources, although they would be limited to using them only during class time.

Suggested Mini-lessons

Because there are so many lessons and instructions required for writing a research paper, we have included this section to aid you in giving the *mini-lessons* suggested on the time line.

Research Skills

For this mini-lesson, we usually had our librarian go over the skills needed for researching materials in the library. She would cover information such as using reference books; how to look up information on the computer database using the subject, author, or title; and special library services (such as interlibrary loans or special collections). In fifth grade, we did not go over using periodical indexes, but that is a skill from which older students would certainly benefit.

Bibliography Card Format

Refer to the reproducible page titled "Sample Bibliography Cards" when going over this mini-lesson. This reproducible shows the students how to set up their bibliography cards for the type of reference material they are using (book, encyclopedia, or magazine). If students found information on a computer encyclopedia, they should follow the encyclopedia format as closely as possible. For information taken from the Internet, they should list the Web site (beginning with www.) and underline the entire name.

When going over this material with the students, have them pay close attention to the way each line is punctuated. The punctuation on the card is written in the correct format for the bibliography page. We required that they use one line for each piece of information (author, title, city, etc.) to make it easy to see whether or not the appropriate information was included (see Figure 7.1).

Figure 7.1   Bibliography Card

Student's Name	**A**
Author's name (Last name, First name.)	
<u>Book Title</u>.	
City published:	
Publishing company,	
Copyright year.	

Also, it is very important that they assign each card a letter from the alphabet, beginning with the letter A. This will be needed for maintaining organization, as explained in more detail in the note card mini-lesson.

Bibliography Page

Refer to the reproducible titled "Sample Bibliography Page" when going over this mini-lesson. Items to emphasize with the students are the following:

1. The title, "Bibliography," should be at the top of the page and centered.

2. Sources must be in alphabetical order, using the authors' last names. If there is no author listed (as with an encyclopedia), alphabetize by the title of the article.

3. The punctuation and spacing should follow the format on the reproducible (skip lines between sources; if the information takes more than one line, the second and third lines should be indented).

Note Card Format and Plagiarism

Refer to the reproducible titled "Sample Note Card Format" when going over this mini-lesson. There are six items the students are required to include on their note cards:

1. *Subject:* In the upper left-hand corner of the card, the students should write the subject on which they are taking notes. These will be primarily the topics on which the students are researching (classification, size, location, care of young, etc.). This will be necessary for organizing their notes once they are ready to work on their rough drafts.

2. *Source card letter:* In the upper right-hand corner of the card, the students should label the source card letter from which the notes are taken. For example, the note cards written from Source C should all have a "C" in the upper right-hand corner.

3. *Source card number:* Following the source card letter, the student should have each note card numbered, beginning with number "1" for each source (e.g., A-1, A-2, A-3; B-1, B-2, B-3). This serves three purposes. First of all, it simplifies finding the total number of cards the students wrote without having to count each card. Second, it makes it easy for the students to put their cards in order if they drop them or somehow mix them up. Finally, there is never a question about which source a note card is from when it is taken out of context.

4. *Page number(s):* On the bottom right-hand corner of the card, students should write the page number(s) from which they took their notes. This will be needed when citing information in their reports.

5. *Student's name:* On the bottom left-hand corner of the card, students should write their names (and possibly their class period). This simplifies finding the owner of a lost card if a student drops one in class or leaves one in a classroom reference book.

6. *Notes:* The center of the card is where the students should write their notes. It is important to emphasize that if they copy information word for word from one of their sources, they need to write it in quotation marks on their cards. This would also be the time to discuss with the students about what *plagiarism* is (presenting someone else's words or ideas as if they were your own), and how they can avoid it through proper citation of their research material.

Outline Format

Refer to the reproducible titled "Outline Example" when going over this mini-lesson. Items to emphasize with the students are the following:

1. The title, "Outline," should be at the top of the page and centered.

2. Go over the proper format for an outline:
   a. Indent topics (do not overlap).
   b. Begin with roman numerals, followed by capital letters, followed by numbers, followed by lowercase letters, and so on.
   c. If there is an "A," there must be a "B"; if there is a "1," there must be a "2," and so on.
   d. The outline should not be written in complete sentences but in words or phrases.
   e. The first Roman numeral on the outline should be the introduction, and the last one should be the conclusion.

At this time, we would have the students take all their note cards (from *every* source) and group them according to the subjects written in the top left-hand corner of the card. For example, all the cards on "size" from each source would be grouped together, all the cards on "location" from each source would be grouped together, and so forth. When students did this, they could easily see how their cards were grouped into related topics and subtopics, and the outline would simply fall into place. We had students set up one paragraph (or Roman numeral) per required research topic. The subtopics became their capital letters (A, B, C, etc), and the details on their notes became the numbers (1, 2, 3, etc.).

Citing Quotes

When having students cite their sources within the text of their report, we required that they use parentheses and list the author's last name and page number. There are many ways to cite information. Use the format you are most comfortable with. We had students punctuate their citations as follows:

Introductory statement, "direct quotation from reference material" (author's last name, page number).

Using the Outline and Note Cards to Write the Rough Draft

Once the students have their outlines written and their note cards grouped into topics and subtopics, writing the report is just a matter of lining up the two and going from there. Students should write to present the researched information in their own voice, being certain to cite their sources throughout the text.

How to Evaluate the Sources of Reference

Points should be assigned as follows:

a. *Used at least four sources of reference, with not more than two encyclopedias, to gather information* (5 points): 1 point for each source and 1 point for not having more than two encyclopedias.

b. *Bibliography cards were written on each source according to the format provided in class* (5 points): 1 point for each source card and 1 point for using the correct format (as explained on the reproducible page).

How to Evaluate the Note Cards

Points should be assigned as follows:

a. *Turned in twenty-five or more note cards* (25 points): 1 point per note card.

b. *Followed the format provided in class for taking notes on cards* (10 points): 2 points for including each of the following in the proper place on each card (see Figure 7.2):
   1) subject
   2) source card letter and number
   3) page number
   4) student's name
   5) notes

c. *Gathered information on all topics required for the paper* (10 points): 2 points for each subject that the student has note cards for (some students may not find information about whether or not their topic is endangered; do not take off points if they do not have that in their notes).

Figure 7.2   Note Card

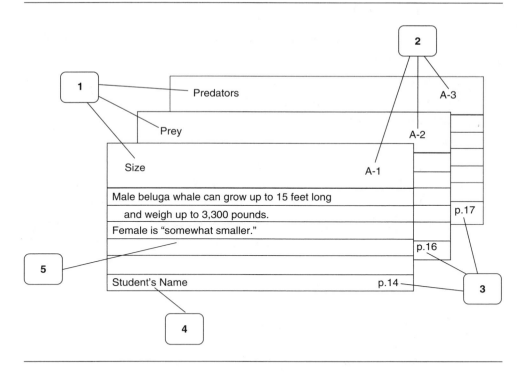

d. *Gathered information from all four sources* (5 points): 1 point for having note cards on each of the required four sources and 1 point for properly grouping the note cards behind the bibliography card it belongs to.

How to Evaluate the Outline

a. *Written in proper outline format including an introduction and conclusion* (10 points): "Outline" title is centered at the top of the page (1 point); indented properly (2 points); used the correct format of Roman numerals, followed by capital letters, followed by numbers (2 points); did not have an "A" without a "B" (1 point); did not write the outline in complete sentences (2 points); included an introduction and conclusion (2 points).

b. *Included all required information* (10 points): once again, that is basically 2 points per requirement.

How to Evaluate the Rough Draft

a. *Followed Composition Book Guidelines* (10 points): 1 point per guideline.

b. *Followed the outline format* (10 points): on a scale of 1 to 10, how well did the student's rough draft follow the outline?

c. *Included 300 words or more* (5 points): deduct 1 point for every ten words below 300.

d. *Included all the required information* (10 points): once again, that is basically 2 points per requirement.

e. *Sources were cited properly* (5 points): 1 point for using each properly: parentheses, the author's last name, the page number, quotation marks, punctuation.

f. *Included a bibliography page using proper format* (10 points): title at the top and center of the page (2 points), sources cited in alphabetical order by the author's last name (4 points), punctuated and spaced properly (4 points).

g. *Was informative and interesting to read* (10 points): on a scale of 1 to 10, how informative and interesting was it to read?

How to Evaluate the Final Draft

When evaluating the students' final drafts, points should be assigned as follows:

a. *Used correct spelling, punctuation, and grammar* (10 points): spelling (3 points), punctuation (4 points), and grammar (3 points).

b. *Corrections from conference were made* (10 points): on a scale of 1 to 10, how well did the student make the revisions discussed during your conference?

c. *Followed the outline format* (10 points): on a scale of 1 to 10, how well did the student's final draft follow the outline?

d. *Neatness and care were taken in publication* (10 points): on a scale of 1 to 10, was the final copy neat, easy to read, and typed or written in cursive (in black or blue ink only)?

e. *Designed and included a creative cover for the report* (5 points): on a scale of 1 to 5, how creative was the cover the student designed? Did it include the title of the report and the student's name?

f. *The final report was submitted in the correct order (cover, outline, report, and bibliography)* (10 points): 2 points for each requirement included, and 2 points for having them in the correct order.

Modifying the Rubric

This assignment can be used with virtually any research topic. How to evaluate it could remain the same, as long as you maintain the basic format requirements. To use this rubric for any other research paper, all you would have to do is rework the top half that states what the paper is to be about and what information it should include.

STUDENT EXAMPLES

Outline Example by Kiley Kartchner

Figure 7.3

$2^5/25$ Outline of Giant Squid

I.   Introduction
     A. Giant Squid
     B. Physical Characteristics
          1. eight tenticles with two feeding tenticles
          2. ring suckers are all around tenticles
          3. eyes are as big as headlights on a automobile
     C. Why- thought it was cool to study
II. Classification
     A. invertebrate
     B. biggest invatebrate there is

III. Size
     A. record breaker was eighteen meters long
     B. average is thirteen meters long

IV. Location
     A. oceans near New Zeland
     B. 1,000 to 3,000 feet down in sea
     C. scientists arent sure how deep

Figure 7.3 (Continued)

1. washed on beach
2. caught in fishing nets
3. floating on surface of sea

V. Care of Young (COMMON Squid)
   A Eggs are torpedo shaped
   B. Mother lives mainly one year
      1. Mother lays eggs
      2. Mother mostly dies
      3. Has 100 eggs to lay

VI.   Position of the food chain
     A. Prey
       1. cuttle fish
       2. bottle nose dolphin
       3. Hammer Head Sharks
       4. Whales
     B. Predator
       1. Sperm Whale

VII. Endangered?
    A. Not endangered
    B. Mother lays 100 eggs (common squid)

VIII. Conclusion
    A. Took a while to learn
    B. Fun to study
    C. I feel like squids are interesting

Rough Draft Example by Samantha Phelps

Figure 7.4

It's *means it is*

slender, and without a ~~stingu~~ stinger

It's body is diamond-shaped, and it's

has two identical lobes (like horns)

on either side of its mouth.

The Manta ray is a ~~vertebrae~~ vertebrate.

Its bones are like sharks bones;

made of ~~cartalige~~ cartilage. ~~Cartalige~~ Cartilage bones

are very helpful to the manta

because they ~~make~~ help it go faster

~~A manta's bones are very flexible~~

It's
~~A manta's~~ flexible bones help

Excerpts From Several Students' Final Drafts

Introduction and paragraph on classification

By Laura Perea

I am doing my research report on the Portuguese Man-of-War. I chose it because it sounded interesting. The Portuguese Man-of-War looks like a jellyfish and has the same physical characteristics. It has many long, poisonous tentacles. Most Men-of-War are either blue, green, or purple.

The Portuguese Man-of-War is an invertebrate. It does not have a backbone. In fact, it has no bones at all! The Man-of-War and the jellyfish have no bones and no brains. Pretty much the only difference between the two sea creatures is that the jellyfish is made of one organism, and the Man-of-War is four different organisms.

Paragraph on size

By Samantha Phelps

A manta is really big, almost gigantic! Its wingspan can get up to 20 feet long, but the average wingspan is 15 to 18 feet long. Its weight is about 3,000 pounds or so, but one manta was recorded to weigh 1.5 tons!. . . .

Paragraph on location

By Joel Kent

Hammerheads like tropical waters. They are located in the Pacific Ocean, off the coast of Hawaii. They also can be found off the coast of Australia, and in the Atlantic Ocean. Some can be found off the eastern coast of the United States.

Paragraph on how it takes care of its young

By John Perea

Sea Turtles do not take care of their young. In fact, the only protection mother Sea Turtles give to their babies is when they bury the eggs! Mother Sea Turtles probably never see their babies. They lay their eggs, bury them and then head for the sea. A few months later, the newborn Sea Turtles must hatch and then try to survive on their own.

Paragraph on position in the food chain

By Holly Twitchell

Harp seals are both prey and predators, but mainly prey, because they are hunted by 4 animals: Polar Bears, Greenland Sharks, Killer Whales, and sealers. Sealers are people who kill harp seal pups for their fluffy white fur. Harp seals eat fish, and other animals too.

Paragraph on if it is endangered

By Joel Kent

Hammerhead sharks are not endangered. They don't have many natural enemies. Their only enemies are humans and bigger sharks. Bigger sharks eat smaller sharks. Stronger sharks eat weaker sharks. Sharks were used for fishmeal, liver oil, and leather products.

Paragraph on other interesting facts

By Samantha Phelps

These are some other information I found out about Manta Rays. The word "manta" means, "Blanket" in Spanish, so that explains the manta's shape and name. A Manta Ray sometimes leaps 15 feet into the air, but not when cleaner fish or remoras are attached to it. Another thing is that mantas are not a threat to the human race, they are just harmless and curious.

Conclusion

By John Perea

Sea turtles should be nicknamed "The Mysteries of the Sea," because of the strange things that they do. Scientists need to study Sea Turtles more because there is so much we don't know about them. Sea Turtles are cool. Maybe someday they will flourish like they once did.

Name: _____

RESEARCH PAPER RUBRIC

Ocean Life

For your next writing project, you will be writing a research paper on some form of animal life that lives in or near oceans. A topic will be chosen in class. The following information must be included in your research:

1. Classification (vertebrate or invertebrate)

2. Its size

3. Location (what oceans it lives in or near)

4. How it takes care of its young

5. Position in the food chain (prey and predators)

6. If it is endangered

The topic you have chosen is: _____

The following items will constitute your final grade on your research project:

1. <u>Sources of Reference</u>: (Worth 10 points: _____)

   Due: _____

Grades will be based on the following:

   a. Used at least four sources of reference, with not more than two encyclopedias, to gather information (5 points)
   b. Bibliography cards were written on each source according to the format provided in class (5 points)

2. <u>Note Cards</u>: (Worth 50 points: _____)

   Due: _____

Grades will be based on the following:

   a. Turned in twenty-five or more note cards (25 points)
   b. Followed the format provided in class for taking notes on cards (10 points)
   c. Gathered information on all topics required for the paper (10 points)
   d. Gathered information from all four sources (5 points)

3. <u>Outline</u>: (Worth 20 points: _____)

    Due: _____

Grades will be based on the following:

 a. Written in proper outline format including an introduction and conclusion (10 points)
 b. Included all required information (10 points)

4. <u>Rough Draft</u>: (Worth 60 points: _____)

    Due: _____

Grades will be based on the following:

 a. Followed Composition Book Guidelines (10 points)
 b. Followed the outline format (10 points)
 c. Included 300 words or more (5 points)
 d. Included all the required information (10 points)
 e. Sources were cited properly (5 points)
 f. Included a bibliography page using proper format (10 points)
 g. Was informative and interesting to read (10 points)

5. <u>Conference</u>:

Before you begin work on your final draft, you and I must conference about your rough draft. We will discuss all the skills you used well along with skills that need improvement. We will both keep track of these skills to help measure your improvement in writing.

6. <u>Final Draft</u>: (Worth 55 points: _____)

    Due: _____

Grades will be based on the following:

 a. Used correct spelling, punctuation, and grammar (10 points)
 b. Corrections from conference were made (10 points)
 c. Followed the outline format (10 points)
 d. Neatness and care were taken in publication (10 points)
 e. Designed and included a creative cover for the report (5 points)
 f. The final report was submitted in the correct order (cover, outline, report, and bibliography) (10 points)

7. Presentation: (Worth 5 points: _____)

    Due: _____

When presenting your research paper, you will be graded on your eye contact, volume, clarity, posture, and pride (1 point for each).

Please cut and return the bottom portion to your teacher. Keep the top portion in your writing folder.

Research Report Writing Rubric

Student Contract

I understand the writing assignment for which I am responsible. I will turn in my work by the required due dates, being careful to include all mandatory components of this assignment. I understand that anything not completed in class will become homework.

Student signature: _____   Date: _____

7. <u>Presentation</u>: (Worth 5 points: _____)

Due: _____

When presenting your research paper, you will be graded on your eye contact, volume, clarity, posture, and pride (1 point for each).

Please cut and return the bottom portion to your teacher. Keep the top portion in your writing folder.

Research Report Writing Rubric

Student Contract With Parent Signature

I understand the writing assignment for which I am responsible. I will turn in my work by the required due dates, being careful to include all mandatory components of this assignment. I understand that anything not completed in class will become homework.

Student signature: _____   Date: _____

I am aware of the writing assignment for which my child is responsible as well as the due dates for each part. I understand that anything not completed in class will become homework.

Parent signature: _____   Date: _____

TOPIC LIST

Dolphin	Puffin
Eels	Royal Albatross
Horseshoe Crab	Sea Gull
Krill	Sea Horse
Lobster	Seal
Manatee	Sea Otter
Manta Ray	Sea Turtle
Marlin	Sharks
Octopus	Shrimp
Pelican	Squid
Penguin	Starfish
Polar Bear	Swordfish
Porcupine Fish	Tuna
Porpoise	Walrus
Portuguese Man-of-War	Whales

SAMPLE BIBLIOGRAPHY CARDS

Write your name on each card.

Assign letters to each source card, beginning with letter A, and label each card in the upper right-hand corner.

Student's Name   Book Format   **A**

Author's name (Last name, First name.)

Book Title.

City published:

Publishing company,

Copyright year.

Student's Name   Encyclopedia Format   **B**

Article author's name (if listed). (Last name, First name.)

"Title of Article."

Title of Encyclopedia.

Edition.

Copyright year.

Student's Name   Magazine Format   **C**

Article author's name (Last name, First name.)

"Title of Article."

Title of Magazine.

Date of publication: (day, month, year:)

Pages of the article.

SAMPLE BIBLIOGRAPHY PAGE

"Beluga (whale)." <u>Grolier Multimedia Encyclopedia</u>. Version 7.0.2. 1995.

Prevost, John F. <u>Beluga Whales</u>. Minneapolis: Library bound edition distributed by Rockbottom Books, 1995.

Watson, Jane Werner. <u>Whales: Friendly Dolphins and Mighty Giants of the Sea</u>. New York: Western Publishing Company, Inc., 1975.

www.enchantedlearning.com/subjects/whales/species/beluga.shtml

<u>Zoobooks: Whales</u>. San Diego, CA: Wildlife Education, Ltd., 1996.

SAMPLE NOTE CARD FORMAT

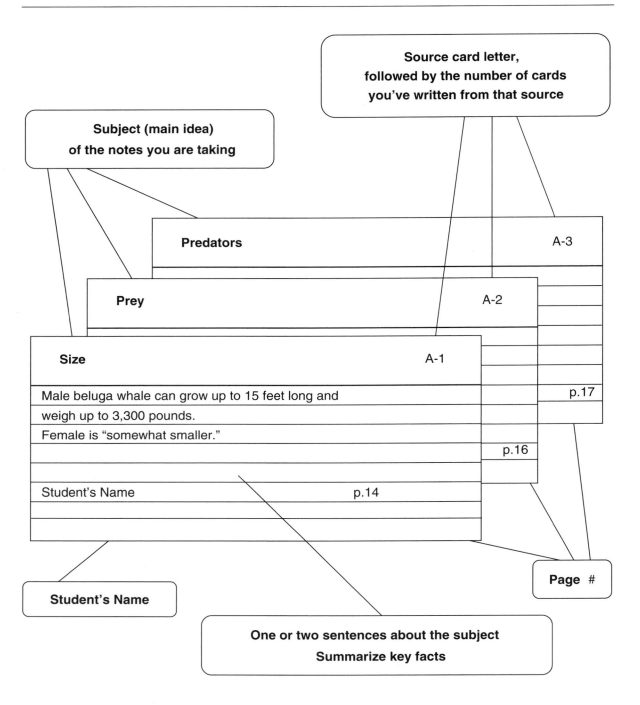

Source card letter,
followed by the number of cards
you've written from that source

Subject (main idea)
of the notes you are taking

Predators   A-3

Prey   A-2

Size   A-1

Male beluga whale can grow up to 15 feet long and   p.17
weigh up to 3,300 pounds.
Female is "somewhat smaller."
                                                      p.16
Student's Name   p.14

Student's Name

One or two sentences about the subject
Summarize key facts

Page #

Note: If you copy a section of text word for word from one of your sources, put
it in quotation marks.

OUTLINE EXAMPLE

I. Introduction
   A. Beluga whale
   B. Physical characteristics
      1. Black to bluish color at birth
      2. Creamy white in about five years
      3. Large head

II. Classification
   A. Vertebrate
      1. Helps support large body
      2. Allows agility in water
   B. Monodontidae (family)
   C. Cetacea (order)

III. Size
   A. Length of up to 15 feet
   B. Weighs up to 3,300 pounds
   C. Females are somewhat smaller than males

IV. Location
   A. Arctic Ocean
   B. Neighboring seas

V. Care of young
   A. Mother
      1. Takes up to 14 months to deliver one "baby"
      2. Nurses for several months
   B. Travels in small family groups

VI. Position in food chain
   A. Prey
      1. Bottom dwelling fish
      2. Other sea life
      3. Uses echolocation to detect prey
   B. Predators
      1. Polar bears
      2. Humans

VII. Endangered?
   A. Not endangered
   B. Once exploited
   C. Now fished commercially under regulated limits

VIII. Conclusion

Name: _____

RESEARCH PAPER ROUGH DRAFT GRADING RUBRIC

Followed Composition Book Guidelines .... worth 10 points: _____

Followed the outline format .... worth 10 points: _____

Contained at least 300 words..................................... worth 5 points: _____

Included all the required information .... worth 10 points: _____

Sources were cited properly .... worth 5 points: _____

Included a bibliography page using proper format...... worth 10 points: _____

Was informative and interesting to read..................... worth 10 points: _____

Worth 60 points: _____

Percentage/Letter Grade: _____

Name: _____

RESEARCH PAPER FINAL DRAFT
AND PRESENTATION GRADING RUBRIC

Used correct spelling, punctuation, and grammar .... worth 10 points: _____

Corrections from conference were made.................... worth 10 points: _____

Followed the outline format .... worth 10 points: _____

Neatness and care were taken in publication .... worth 10 points: _____

Designed and included a creative cover for the
report... worth 5 points: _____

The final report was submitted in the correct order...... worth 10 points: _____

Presentation: eye contact, volume, clarity, posture,
and pride .... worth 5 points: _____

Worth 60 points: _____

Percentage/Letter Grade: _____

8

News Article

TEACHER INSTRUCTION
FOR NEWS ARTICLE RUBRIC

Suggested Timeline

	Monday	Tuesday	Wednesday	Thursday	Friday
Week 1	Read and summarize *Mini-lesson	Introduce Rubric	Research	Research	Research
Week 2	Pre-write is due				Rough Draft is due Conferences
Week 3	Conferences			Final Draft is due Presentations	Presentations

*Parts of an article.

Handouts Provided for This Assignment

News article rubric (three pages)

Parts of a news article (one page)

List of possible topics (one page)

Rough draft and final draft/presentation grading rubrics (one page)

Other Materials Needed

News articles (from *Scholastic News*, *Weekly Reader*, the newspaper, etc.)

Introducing the Rubric

Prior to introducing the rubric, it would be helpful to spend a class period with the students reading and summarizing news articles. Younger students could work from *Scholastic News* or *Weekly Reader*, while older students could use a regular newspaper. This would be the time to focus instruction on the parts of a news article (headline, byline, lead, quote, body, and ending) using the reproducible page provided. Have the students read the articles they have chosen, looking for the news article parts described on the reproducible page. An entire class period could be spent on this, discussing what elements the writers used to make their articles more interesting.

When introducing the rubric, read it aloud to the class section by section, answering any questions the students may have as you go along. Have students fill in the due dates for each part of the process in the spaces provided on the rubric. Students should also fill in the due dates for each part of the process in their assignment books.

Students should be able to pick their topics on the day you introduce the rubric. We have provided you with a list of possible topics to use as an overhead transparency. These are only suggestions, and you are certainly not limited to them. A strategy we found both helpful and fair for situations like this was to have students' names on craft sticks placed in a cup. The person whose name was drawn first got first choice from the topic list, whereas the student whose name was drawn last received the last choice. We tried to provide more topics than there were students so that even the last student had a choice. There was never a question on fairness when we did this. (Note: we had students work in pairs for this assignment because of the scope of the project we were working on in class. See the Publishing Suggestion section in this chapter for more information.)

Students will also need some time to research their topics before working on their pre-writes. You might spend a class period visiting the school library for research material, or you could check out a variety of books for reference in the classroom. Whatever you choose to do, give students ample time to learn about their topics before the pre-write is due.

How to Evaluate the Pre-writing

The pre-writing is worth 5 points. That breaks down to 1 point for each element that is properly clustered or outlined according to the questions provided on the rubric.

How to Evaluate the Rough Draft

When evaluating the students' rough drafts, points should be assigned as follows:

a. *Followed Composition Book Guidelines* (10 points): 1 point for following each guideline.

b. *Written with at least 200 words* (10 points): deduct 2 points for every ten words below 200.

c. *Included the "who, what, when, where, why, and how"* (10 points): who and what (1 point each); when, where, why, and how (2 points each).

d. *Written in news article format: headline, byline, lead, quote, body, and ending* (10 points): byline and quote (1 point each); headline, lead, body, and ending (2 points each).

e. *Made it clear what the situation was and how it occurred* (10 points): on a scale of 1 to 10, was the student clear in what the situation was and how it occurred?

f. *Was creative yet realistic* (10 points): on a scale of 1 to 10, was the article both creative and realistic?

How to Evaluate the Final Draft

When evaluating the students' final drafts, points should be assigned as follows:

a. *Used correct spelling, punctuation, and grammar* (10 points): spelling (3 points), punctuation (4 points), and grammar (3 points).

b. *Corrections from conference were made* (10 points): on a scale of 1 to 10, how well did the student make the revisions discussed during your conference?

c. *Neatness and care were taken in publication* (10 points): on a scale of 1 to 10, was the final copy neat, easy to read, and typed or written in cursive (in black or blue ink only)?

Publishing Suggestion

When we required students to write these news articles, we were involved in a thematic study of ecology. This assignment was actually a smaller portion of a multimedia project they were involved with during our computer lab time. We instructed students on determining column width; how to copy, cut, and paste information and text; transferring graphics from other programs; and using the Internet for more information. These articles were then published in the form of a newspaper, *The Ecological Times*, in which students were also responsible for one other "special topic" found in most newspapers:

editorials	sports	interviews	movie reviews
surveys	weather	classified ads	advertisements
recipes	comics	horoscopes	puzzles/games
advice column	editor*		

Because of the scope of this project, we had students work in pairs to write the articles and then each be responsible for one special topic. We limited "weather," "horoscopes," and "advice column" to only one student, while all others were limited to not more than two or three, depending on the number of students in our class. We challenged students to be creative in relating their special topic to our theme of ecology.

*Some students, instead of working on special topics, worked as editors. They were responsible for working with a small group of students in designing and setting up the layout of their section of the newspaper. We had three sections to our paper, and therefore had three editors.

We found the results from our fifth graders incredible! Imagine the possibilities of what you could do with higher grade levels.

Modifying the Rubric

The possibilities on how you could use this assignment are endless. The format stays the same, regardless of the focal area of study. It can be used with any science strand, as we used it with our study of ecology. Or you could have students research and write about any event or time period in history, from the perspective of that time period. It is important to remember that anything you require the students to do must be stated in the rubric. Therefore, the points and requirements would have to be adjusted.

Name: _____

NEWS ARTICLE RUBRIC

For your next assignment in writing, you will be creating a news article informing others of an ecological situation in the world today. You will need to research your topic before starting your pre-write. You will be required to follow the writing process for this, and grades will be based on the following:

1. Pre-write: (Worth 5 points: _____)

    Due: _____

This should outline what you plan to include in your article based on your research. Your article should include the following information:

  a. The situation
  b. How the situation occurred
  c. Ways to prevent further problems
  d. Any other interesting facts related to the situation

As in any news article, it will be important to have the "who, what, when, where, why, and how" stated in the article.

2. Rough Draft: (Worth 60 points: _____)

    Due: _____

Your rough draft will be graded as follows:

  a. Followed Composition Book Guidelines (10 points)
  b. Written with at least 200 words (10 points)
  c. Included the "who, what, when, where, why, and how" (10 points)
  d. Written in news article format: headline, byline, lead, quote, body, and ending (10 points)
  e. Made it clear what the situation was and how it occurred (10 points)
  f. Was creative yet realistic (10 points)

3. Conference:

Before you begin work on your final draft, you and I must conference about your rough draft. We will discuss all the skills you used well along with skills that need improvement. We will both keep track of these skills to help measure your improvement in writing.

4. <u>Final Draft</u>: (Worth 30 points: _____)

    Due: _____

    Your final draft will be graded as follows:

    a. Used correct spelling, punctuation, and grammar (10 points)
    b. Corrections from conference were made (10 points)
    c. Neatness and care were taken in publication (10 points)

5. <u>Presentation</u>: (Worth 5 points: _____)

    When presenting your news article to the class, you will be graded on the following:

    a. Eye contact: did you look at the audience? (1 point)
    b. Volume: could the audience hear you? (1 point)
    c. Clarity: could the audience understand you? (1 point)
    d. Posture: were you standing straight and tall? (1 point)
    e. Pride: did you sound proud of your work? (1 point)

Please cut and return the bottom portion to your teacher. Keep the top portion in your writing folder.

News Article Writing Rubric

Student Contract

I understand the writing assignment for which I am responsible. I will turn in my work by the required due dates, being careful to include all mandatory components of this assignment. I understand that anything not completed in class will become homework.

Student signature: _____   Date: _____

4. <u>Final Draft</u>: (Worth 30 points: _____)

   Due: _____

Your final draft will be graded as follows:

   a. Used correct spelling, punctuation, and grammar (10 points)
   b. Corrections from conference were made (10 points)
   c. Neatness and care were taken in publication (10 points)

5. <u>Presentation</u>: (Worth 5 points: _____)

When presenting your news article to the class, you will be graded on the following:

   a. Eye contact: did you look at the audience? (1 point)
   b. Volume: could the audience hear you? (1 point)
   c. Clarity: could the audience understand you? (1 point)
   d. Posture: were you standing straight and tall? (1 point)
   e. Pride: did you sound proud of your work? (1 point)

Please cut and return the bottom portion to your teacher. Keep the top portion in your writing folder.

News Article Writing Rubric

Student Contract With Parent Signature

I understand the writing assignment for which I am responsible. I will turn in my work by the required due dates, being careful to include all mandatory components of this assignment. I understand that anything not completed in class will become homework.

Student signature: _____   Date: _____

I am aware of the writing assignment for which my child is responsible as well as the due dates for each part. I understand that anything not completed in class will become homework.

Parent signature: _____   Date: _____

PARTS OF A NEWS ARTICLE

Headline: This is the title of the article. It should be printed in bold type and give the readers a clear idea of what the article is about. It should be creative or "catchy" to get the readers' attention.

Byline: This is the "line" that tells whom the article is written "by." It should be written below the headline and above the article.

Lead: This is the first paragraph of the article. It should briefly state the "who, what, when, where, why, and how" of the news event on which you are reporting. However, it should be written in a way that "leads" the readers into the article, grabs their attention, and leaves them wanting to know more.

Quote: This adds a personal touch to the story. A good quote within the text of the article can make it sound more interesting and true to life.

Body: This is the bulk of the article. It goes into more detail answering the "who, what, when, where, why, and how" of the event.

Ending: This is the last paragraph of the article. It should be written in a way that makes an impact on readers and leaves them with something to think about.

TOPIC LIST

Natural Resources:

    renewable

    nonrenewable

    conservation

Pollution Control:

    water

    air

    land

    noise

    pesticides

Ecosystems:

    wildlife management

    evolution and adaptation of

    forestry

    agriculture

    endangered species

Other Topics:

    reduce, reuse, recycle

    acid rain

    plastics

    landfills

    composting

    greenhouse effect

    rain forests

Name:_____

NEWS ARTICLE ROUGH DRAFT GRADING RUBRIC

Followed Composition Book Guidelines .... worth 10 points: _____

Written with at least 200 words .... worth 10 points: _____

Included the "who, what, when, where, why,
and how" .... worth 10 points: _____

Written in news article format: headline, byline,
lead, quote, body, and ending .... worth 10 points: _____

Made it clear what the situation was and how it
occurred .... worth 10 points: _____

Was creative yet realistic .... worth 10 points: _____

Worth 60 points: _____

Percentage/Letter Grade: _____

Name: _____

NEWS ARTICLE FINAL DRAFT AND
PRESENTATION GRADING RUBRIC

Used correct spelling, punctuation, and
grammar .... worth 10 points: _____

Corrections from conference were made .... worth 10 points: _____

Neatness and care were taken in publication .... worth 10 points: _____

Presentation:
eye contact, volume, clarity, posture, and
pride .... worth 5 points: _____

Worth 35 points: _____

Percentage/Letter Grade: _____

9

Legend

TEACHER INSTRUCTION FOR LEGEND RUBRIC

Suggested Timeline

	Monday	Tuesday	Wednesday	Thursday	Friday
Week 1	Introduce Rubric	Read aloud Legends			Pre-write is due
Week 2					Rough Draft is due
Week 3	Conferences	Conferences			
Week 4				Final Draft is due Presentations	Presentations

Handouts Provided for This Assignment

Legend rubric (three pages)

Rough draft and final draft/presentation grading rubrics (one page)

Other Materials Needed

- Wide variety of legends from the library for reference
- Reference book(s) with book-making ideas (see Resource B)
- Materials for "publishing" student legends: colored pencils or crayons, white paper, construction paper, tag board or poster board (for book covers), scissors, glue, stapler, clear contact paper for a protective cover, and so on.

Introducing the Rubric

The first day of the four-week project should be spent introducing the rubric. Read it aloud to the class section by section, answering any questions the students may have as you go along. Have students fill in the due dates for each part of the process in the space provided on the rubric. Students should also fill in the due dates for each part of the process in their assignment book calendars.

If there is class time available after introducing the rubric, read aloud a legend or two and discuss the elements the authors used. Otherwise, do it the following day. Be sure to give the students some class time to read several legends on their own as well as before they begin working on their pre-writes. This is an important part of the pre-writing experience. Giving students time to do this will help give their stories a more authentic sound.

How to Evaluate the Pre-writing

The pre-writing is worth 5 points. That breaks down to 1 point for each element that is properly clustered or outlined according to the questions provided on the rubric.

How to Evaluate the Rough Draft

When evaluating the students' rough drafts, points should be assigned as follows:

a. *Followed Composition Book Guidelines* (10 points): 1 point for following each guideline.

b. *Written as a legend with appropriate story elements* (10 points): on a scale of 1 to 10, how well was the story written as a legend, and did it include appropriate story elements?

c. *Had a clear beginning, middle, and end* (10 points): beginning (3 points), middle (4 points), and end (3 points). Give students points based on how well each part is developed.

d. *Made sense and was told in a logical order* (5 points): on a scale of 1 to 5, how well did the legend make sense, and was it told in a logical order?

e. *Contained at least 250 words* (5 points): deduct 1 point for every ten words below 250.

When students turn in their rough drafts, they should use their class time to begin work on their book covers, title, and dedication pages. They could also use this time to make decisions on how they are going to "bind" and publish their books. This provides the students with plenty to do while you have their composition books for grading and conferencing.

How to Evaluate the Final Draft

When evaluating the students' final drafts, points should be assigned as follows:

a. *Used correct spelling, punctuation, and grammar* (10 points): spelling (3 points), punctuation (4 points), and grammar (3 points).

b. *Corrections from conference were made* (10 points): on a scale of 1 to 10, how well did the student make the revisions discussed during your conference?

c. *Published in book format: cover, title page, dedication page, and legend* (10 points): 2 points for each requirement and 2 points for having it in the correct order.

d. *Included illustrations, drawn to your best ability, on every page* (10 points): on a scale of 1 to 10, were there illustrations on every page, and were they neat and carefully drawn?

e. *Was neat and easy to read; care was taken in publication* (10 points): on a scale of 1 to 10, was the final copy neat, easy to read, and typed or written in cursive (in black or blue ink only)?

Modifying the Rubric

We used this assignment while studying about Native American culture. However, it could easily be used with the study of any culture's legends or myths. You could also require students to publish them in a particular format (e.g., as a pop-up book). Or you might require students to write on one particular theme or from the perspective of their own cultural background. It is important to remember that anything you require the students to do must be stated in the rubric. Therefore, the points and requirements would have to be adjusted.

STUDENT EXAMPLES

Excerpts From John Perea's Legend, "How Summer Got Her Place"

Figure 9.1 Pre-write

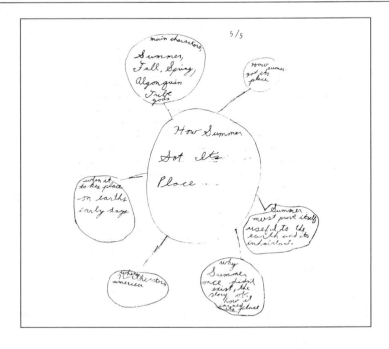

Rough Draft

God was blown away by her beauty. She said,

"My name is Maiden Summer."

"I have come to ask for a place in the year."

The Season God asked.

"Why do you wish to earn this place as a season?"

"Because," She replied, "I have been watching the indian tribes.

They work all year round harvesting and planting. There is no season for relaxation and play."

The Season God became angry with her and sent her away.

Summer promised she would be back to hear his answer.

She left the calm feeling disappeared and the usual cold wind of fall replaced the warm soothing one.

Parts of John's Final Draft

A long time ago during Mother Earth's early days, there were only two seasons – Fall and Spring. For the Gods, this worked fine. But there was one bad thing about this, there being only two seasons the Wacque Indian Tribes had to work all year round. There wasn't any season for play and relaxation, just seasons for harvest and planting.

One day a swirling breeze came over to speak with the Gods. As the warm, soothing breeze got nearer it began to take a young woman's form. . . . When she stepped forward, her beauty blew the giant God away. She said, "My name is Maiden Summer. I have come to ask for a place in the year."

The Season God became angry with her. . . . Then, the mighty God Bellowed, "So be it! You must prove yourself worthy of the place in the year by getting evidence you are needed by the Wacque Tribes."

Summer had no trouble convincing any of the tribes except for one, the Tonsheckeue Tribe. They had a Shaman that led them who liked the way the seasons went just fine. He brushed her away like the wind to a leaf. But She would not give up. She sent a magic soothing breeze into the Shaman's hut. At that moment, the Shaman flew out of his hut. He said, "I have changed my mind!" He gave a cry like a wolf, and began to inform his tribe of his decision.

With that Summer left for the God's kingdom to present her evidence. Thus, after much pleading and begging, she finally got her wish granted. Now we have summer, a season for play and rest, of beautiful sunsets, and warm relaxing days.

The End

Another Student's Final Draft

The Lights of the Sky

By Molly Espinoza

Long ago the earth was a dark place. The sky was just a black blanket that surrounded the earth. The Anasazi were sad. They had food to eat and clothes to wear, but no light or warmth.

The men of the village went in search of these things. The women and children stayed behind. Among the children, a boy named Calling Hawk and his sister Singing Bird thought of nothing but the problem.

The children prayed for the Sky Spirits to come and help them. Their prayer was answered. The Sky Spirits came to them in their dreams. They whispered into Calling Hawk's ear, "In the next five days go to the Silver River and wash your hands and face in it. Then go to Fire Mountain and find the brightest most biggest fire ball you can find. Bring it to the Sacred Rock and throw the ball in the sky, but first take a branch of elm, light it and take it home with you."

In Singing Bird's ear they whispered, "Go to the Field of Gold, take the sharpest blade and dip it in the rain water. Take the blade to Wolf Mountain. Find the biggest boulder and use the blade to cut into it. Then dip it into the water and cover the rock in it. Take it to Sacred Rock."

And from that day they were no longer known as Calling Hawk and Singing Bird, but as Father of the Sun and Mother of the Moon and Stars.

And that is also why Sun is made out of fire and the stars are bright and Moon has craters.

THE END

Name: _____

LEGEND RUBRIC

For this next writing assignment, we will be learning about legends and their use in the Native American culture. As an example, we have included this excerpt from <u>Native American Myths and Legends</u> by Colin F. Taylor, Ph.D.:

> "Indians viewed mankind as but a small, relatively insignificant part of a greater, mysterious universe. They respected the force and power of nature and wove it into their culture. Everywhere, the Indians saw themselves as servants of Mother Earth and Father Sky rather than as their masters. It was a world where animals had a purpose and were respected and acknowledged as creatures of power and deed."

After listening to several legends, you will be given an opportunity to be creative with your own legend writing. Some suggested topics are:

1. How animals came to be and their importance in life

2. How the weather or seasons came to be

3. The reason for the sun, moon, or earth

Your requirements will be as follows:

1. <u>Pre-write</u>: (Worth 5 points: _____)

    Due: _____

In your pre-writing, please include your title and answer the following questions:

   a. When and where does your legend take place?
   b. What is the theme of your legend?
   c. Why is your theme a concern?
   d. How is your problem solved?
   e. Who are your main characters?

2. <u>Rough Draft</u>: (Worth 40 points: _____)

    Due: _____

Your rough draft will be graded as follows:

   a. Followed Composition Book Guidelines (10 points)
   b. Written as a legend with appropriate story elements (10 points)
   c. Had a clear beginning, middle, and end (10 points)
   d. Made sense and was told in a logical order (5 points)
   e. Contained at least 250 words (5 points)

3. <u>Conference</u>:

Before you begin work on your final draft, you and I must conference about your rough draft. We will discuss all the skills you used well along with skills that need improvement. We will both keep track of these skills to help measure your improvement in writing.

4. <u>Final Draft</u>: (Worth 50 points: _____)

   Due: _____

Your final draft will be published into book form. You will be graded as follows:

   a. Correct spelling, punctuation, and grammar were used (10 points)
   b. Corrections from conference were made (10 points)
   c. Published in book format: cover, title page, dedication page, and legend (10 points)
   d. Included illustrations, drawn to your best ability, on every page (10 points)
   e. Was neat and easy to read; care was taken in publication (10 points)

5. <u>Presentation</u>: (Worth 5 points:_____)

You will be required to present your book to the class. You will be graded on:

   a. Eye contact: did you look at the audience? (1 point)
   b. Posture: did you stand straight and tall? (1 point)
   c. Pride: did you read your legend with pride? (1 point)
   d. Volume: could the audience hear you? (1 point)
   e. Clarity: could the audience understand you? (1 point)

Please cut and return the bottom portion to your teacher. Keep the top portion in your writing folder.

Legend Writing Rubric

Student Contract

I understand the writing assignment for which I am responsible. I will turn in my work by the required due dates, being careful to include all mandatory components of this assignment. I understand that anything not completed in class will become homework.

Student signature: _____   Date: _____

3. <u>Conference:</u>

Before you begin work on your final draft, you and I must conference about your rough draft. We will discuss all the skills you used well along with skills that need improvement. We will both keep track of these skills to help measure your improvement in writing.

4. <u>Final Draft:</u> (Worth 50 points: _____)

   Due: _____

Your final draft will be published into book form. You will be graded as follows:

   a. Correct spelling, punctuation, and grammar were used (10 points)
   b. Corrections from conference were made (10 points)
   c. Published in book format: cover, title page, dedication page, and legend (10 points)
   d. Included illustrations, drawn to your best ability, on every page (10 points)
   e. Was neat and easy to read; care was taken in publication (10 points)

5. <u>Presentation:</u> (Worth 5 points: _____)

You will be required to present your book to the class. You will be graded on:

   a. Eye contact: did you look at the audience? (1 point)
   b. Posture: did you stand straight and tall? (1 point)
   c. Pride: did you read your legend with pride? (1 point)
   d. Volume: could the audience hear you? (1 point)
   e. Clarity: could the audience understand you? (1 point)

Please cut and return the bottom portion to your teacher. Keep the top portion in your writing folder.

Legend Writing Rubric

Student Contract With Parent Signature

I understand the writing assignment for which I am responsible. I will turn in my work by the required due dates, being careful to include all mandatory components of this assignment. I understand that anything not completed in class will become homework.

Student signature: _____   Date: _____

I am aware of the writing assignment for which my child is responsible as well as the due dates for each part. I understand that anything not completed in class will become homework.

Parent signature: _____   Date: _____

Name: _____

LEGEND ROUGH DRAFT GRADING RUBRIC

Followed Composition Book Guidelines................ worth 10 points: _____

Written as a legend with appropriate story
elements .... worth 10 points _____

Had a clear beginning, middle, and end................ worth 10 points: _____

Made sense and was told in a logical order .... worth 5 points: _____

Contained at least 250 words................................. worth 5 points: _____

Worth 40 points: _____

Percentage/Letter Grade: _____

Name: _____

LEGEND FINAL DRAFT AND
PRESENTATION GRADING RUBRIC

Used correct spelling, punctuation, and
grammar .... worth 10 points: _____

Corrections from conference were made................ worth 10 points: _____

Published in book format: cover, title page,
dedication page, and legend .... worth 10 points: _____

Included illustrations on every page .... worth 10 points: _____

Neat and easy to read; care was taken in
publication .... worth 10 points: _____

Presentation:
eye contact, volume, clarity, posture, and
pride .... worth 5 points: _____

Worth 55 points: _____

Percentage/Letter Grade: _____

10

Fairy Tale

TEACHER INSTRUCTION FOR FAIRY TALE RUBRIC

Suggested Timeline

	Monday	Tuesday	Wednesday	Thursday	Friday
Week 1	Introduce Rubric	Read aloud Fairy Tales			Pre-write is due
Week 2					Rough Draft is due
Week 3	Conferences	Conferences			
Week 4				Final Draft is due Presentations	Presentations

Handouts Provided for This Assignment

Fairy tale rubric (three pages)

Rough draft and final draft/presentation grading rubrics (one page)

Other Materials Needed

- Wide variety of fairy tales from the library for reference
- Reference book(s) with book-making ideas (see Resource B)
- Materials for "publishing" student fairy tales: colored pencils or crayons, white paper, construction paper, tag board or poster board (for book covers), scissors, glue, tape, stapler, and so on.

Introducing the Rubric

The first day of the four-week project should be spent introducing the rubric. Read it aloud to the class section by section, answering any questions the students may have as you go along. Have students fill in the due dates for each part of the process in the space provided on the rubric. Students should also fill in the due dates for each part of the process in their assignment book calendars.

If there is class time available after introducing the rubric, read aloud a fairy tale or two and discuss the elements the authors used. Otherwise, do it the following day. Be sure to give the students some class time to read several fairy tales on their own as well as before they begin working on their pre-writes. Giving students time to do this will help give their stories a more authentic sound.

How to Evaluate the Pre-writing

The pre-writing is worth 5 points. That breaks down to 1 point for each element that is properly clustered or outlined according to the questions provided on the rubric.

How to Evaluate the Rough Draft

When evaluating the students' rough drafts, points should be assigned as follows:

a. *Followed Composition Book Guidelines* (10 points): 1 point for following each guideline.

b. *Written as a fairy tale with appropriate story elements* (10 points): on a scale of 1 to 10, how well was the story written as a fairy tale, and did it include appropriate story elements?

c. *Had a clear beginning, middle, and end* (10 points): beginning (3 points), middle (4 points), and end (3 points). Give students points based on how well each part is developed.

d. *Made sense and was told in a logical order* (5 points): on a scale of 1 to 5, how well did the fairy tale make sense, and was it told in a logical order?

e. *Contained at least 250 words* (5 points): deduct 1 point for every five words below 250.

When students turn in their rough drafts, they should use their class time to begin work on their book covers, title pages, and dedication pages. They could also use this time to make decisions on how they are going to "bind" and publish their books. This provides the students with plenty to do while you have their composition books for grading and conferencing.

How to Evaluate the Final Draft

When evaluating the students' final drafts, points should be assigned as follows:

a. *Used correct spelling, punctuation, and grammar* (10 points): spelling (3 points), punctuation (4 points), and grammar (3 points).

b. *Corrections from conference were made* (10 points): on a scale of 1 to 10, how well did the student make the revisions discussed during your conference?

c. *Published in book format: cover, title page, dedication page, and fairy tale* (10 points): 2 points for each requirement and 2 points for having it in the correct order.

d. *Included illustrations, drawn to your best ability, on every page* (10 points): on a scale of 1 to 10, were there illustrations on every page, and were they neat and carefully drawn?

e. *Was neat and easy to read; care was taken in publication* (10 points): on a scale of 1 to 10, was the final copy neat, easy to read, and typed or written in cursive (in black or blue ink only)?

Modifying the Rubric

This assignment could also be given requiring students to create a different version of one particular fairy tale or from a different character's point of view. Another fun assignment would be to have students write a "modern day" version of a fairy tale. You could also require students to publish them in a particular format (for example, as a pop-up book).

If you wanted to add a multicultural twist to your assignment, you could read different versions of the same basic fairy tale (as told from different cultural backgrounds) and require your students to write one on the same theme from the perspective of their own cultural background. You could be very specific on what cultural aspects you would like the students to include in their stories. It is important to remember that anything you require the students to do must be stated in the rubric. Therefore, the points and requirements would have to be adjusted.

STUDENT EXAMPLES

Excerpts From Samantha Phelps's Fairy Tale, "The Three Trials"

Once upon a time there was a land so far and distant, it is said, that land did not even exist. But it did, oh yes, it did. It was called The Blessed Totamna, Land of Magic. Totamna was the most beautiful kingdom anyone had ever seen, though not many had seen it. . . . A kindhearted Princess named Rosette ruled over this joyful kingdom. Rosette, like her kingdom, was a very beautiful young lady, with her long golden hair and electric blue eyes she looked like an angel. She was also very cunning and tricky, but had well manners when it was needed.

Princess Rosette became very tired as she tramped along through the forest most of the day, but at sunset, she finally found the castle of the Goblins. She went boldly up to the big brass door and knocked. The old door creaked slowly open, and Rosette then with caution, stepped inside the dull gray Lair.

The Seven High Counselors edged forward and were about to speak when a gruff, deep, broken voice cut them off. The voice belonged to a green and scaly monster with dark hair sprouting from his ears like a fountain. He was fairly gigantic, and with a breath that smelled of rotten, melted cheese. His teeth looked remotely like cracked fangs, and they were yellow and crawling with fungus. Rosette recognized him as the Goblin King himself!

Rosette was pale with nervousness. She didn't know what to think. A Goblin King kept a dishrag as a servant? He would give her three trials, and if she passed them, her village would live in peace? This King was mad! Even more mad because he kept howling Goblins inside his castle!

Princess Rosette was smart and fast, so she knew straight away that only a song would tame a lion. She started singing with a voice like a mockingbird in spring. She sang so sweet and soft that not only the lion became drowsy, but the Goblin crowd, too, became sleepy. All the court was sleeping by the time Rosette's song was over. The Goblin King, though, was not asleep, but deeply impressed.

. . . . "Thank you for keeping your promise, Goblin!"

With renewed confidence, Rosette then walked the two-day journey back to her kingdom.

****

As soon as Princess Rosette arrived, her village burst with joy and applause. Rosette was then, and forever will be named Her Majesty, Queen Rosette! And, well, you know the gig . . .

They lived happily ever after!

Name: _____

FAIRY TALE RUBRIC

Fairy Tales are stories that often tell a tale of good versus evil using both human and fictitious characters. Many times fairy tales include magical events, the number three or seven, or there is repetition in either dialogue or setting. They often include an implied moral as well. After hearing several fairy tales in class, you will be required to write your own. Be sure to include these fairy tale elements in your story. There are five steps you will need to complete for this writing assignment. They are:

    1. <u>Pre-write</u>: (Worth 5 points: _____)

        Due: _____

You must do some form of pre-writing or brainstorming to show that you have thought your story through. A good place to start is by answering the questions:

        a. When and where does the story take place?
        b. Who and what are the main characters?
        c. What is the conflict of good vs. evil?
        d. How is the conflict resolved?
        e. What other fairy tale elements will you include?

    2. <u>Rough Draft</u>: (Worth 40 points: _____)

        Due: _____

Your rough draft will be graded as follows:

        a. Followed Composition Book Guidelines (10 points)
        b. Written as a fairy tale with appropriate story elements (10 points)
        c. Had a clear beginning, middle, and end (10 points)
        d. Made sense and was told in a logical order (5 points)
        e. Contained at least 250 words (5 points)

    3. <u>Conference</u>:

Before you begin work on your final draft, you and I must conference about your rough draft. We will discuss all the skills you used well along with skills that need improvement. We will both keep track of these skills to help measure your improvement in writing.

4. <u>Final Draft</u>: (Worth 50 points: _____)

   Due: _____

You must rewrite your story in a neat final copy that will be published into book form. From your rough draft, you will need to make decisions about where to separate your writing for each page, what kinds of illustrations you want, as well as where you want them. Your final draft will be graded as follows:

   a. Correct spelling, punctuation, and grammar were used (10 points)
   b. Corrections from conference were made (10 points)
   c. Published in book format: cover, title page, dedication page, and story (10 points)
   d. Included illustrations, drawn to your best ability, on every page (10 points)
   e. Neat and easy to read; care was taken in publication (10 points)

5. <u>Presentation</u>: (Worth 5 points: _____)

   Due: _____

When presenting your fairy tale to the class, you will be graded on the following:

   a. Eye contact: did you look at the audience? (1 point)
   b. Volume: could the audience hear you? (1 point)
   c. Clarity: could the audience understand you? (1 point)
   d. Posture: were you standing straight and tall? (1 point)
   e. Pride: did you sound proud of your work? (1 point)

Please cut and return the bottom portion to your teacher. Keep the top portion in your writing folder.

Fairy Tale Writing Rubric

Student Contract

I understand the writing assignment for which I am responsible. I will turn in my work by the required due dates, being careful to include all mandatory components of this assignment. I understand that anything not completed in class will become homework.

Student signature: _____   Date: _____

4. <u>Final Draft</u>: (Worth 50 points: _____)

    Due: _____

You must rewrite your story in a neat final copy that will be published into book form. From your rough draft, you will need to make decisions about where to separate your writing for each page, what kinds of illustrations you want, as well as where you want them. Your final draft will be graded as follows:

    a. Correct spelling, punctuation, and grammar were used (10 points)
    b. Corrections from conference were made (10 points)
    c. Published in book format: cover, title page, dedication page, and story (10 points)
    d. Included illustrations, drawn to your best ability, on every page (10 points)
    e. Neat and easy to read; care was taken in publication (10 points)

5. <u>Presentation</u>: (Worth 5 points: _____)

    Due: _____

When presenting your fairy tale to the class, you will be graded on the following:

    a. Eye contact: did you look at the audience? (1 point)
    b. Volume: could the audience hear you? (1 point)
    c. Clarity: could the audience understand you? (1 point)
    d. Posture: were you standing straight and tall? (1 point)
    e. Pride: did you sound proud of your work? (1 point)

Please cut and return the bottom portion to your teacher. Keep the top portion in your writing folder.

Fairy Tale Writing Rubric

Student Contract With Parent Signature

I understand the writing assignment for which I am responsible. I will turn in my work by the required due dates, being careful to include all mandatory components of this assignment. I understand that anything not completed in class will become homework.

Student signature: _____ Date: _____

I am aware of the writing assignment for which my child is responsible as well as the due dates for each part. I understand that anything not completed in class will become homework.

Parent signature: _____ Date: _____

Name: _____

FAIRY TALE ROUGH DRAFT GRADING RUBRIC

Followed Composition Book Guidelines .... worth 10 points: _____

Written as a fairy tale with appropriate story
elements .... worth 10 points: _____

Had a clear beginning, middle, and end .... worth 10 points: _____

Made sense and was told in a logical order .... worth 5 points: _____

Contained at least 250 words .... worth 5 points: _____

Worth 40 points: _____

Percentage/Letter Grade: _____

Name: _____

FAIRY TALE FINAL DRAFT AND
PRESENTATION GRADING RUBRIC

Used correct spelling, punctuation, and grammar... worth 10 points:_____

Corrections from conference were made .... worth 10 points: _____

Published in book format: cover, title page,
dedication page, and story .... worth 10 points: _____

Included illustrations on every page .... worth 10 points: _____

Neat and easy to read; care was taken in
publication .... worth 10 points:_____

Presentation:
eye contact, volume, clarity, posture, pride .... worth 5 points: _____

Worth 55 points: _____

Percentage/Letter Grade: _____

11

Science Fiction

TEACHER INSTRUCTION FOR SCIENCE FICTION RUBRIC

Suggested Timeline

	Monday	Tuesday	Wednesday	Thursday	Friday
Week 1	Introduce Rubric				Pre-write is due
Week 2					Rough Draft is due
Week 3	Conferences	Conferences			
Week 4				Final Draft is due Presentations	Presentations

Handouts Provided for This Assignment

Science fiction rubric (three pages)

Rough draft and final draft/presentation grading rubrics (one page)

Other Materials Needed

- Reference book(s) with book-making ideas (see Resource B)
- Materials for "publishing" student science fiction stories: colored pencils or crayons, white paper, construction paper, tag board or poster board (for book covers), scissors, glue, tape, stapler, and so on.

Introducing the Rubric

The first day of the four-week project should be spent introducing the rubric. Read it aloud to the class section by section, answering any questions the students may have as you go along. Have students fill in the due dates for each part of the process in the space provided on the rubric. Students should also fill in the due dates for each part of the process in their assignment book calendars.

The reading and writing connection is an important one for students to realize. During the time that students were working on this writing project, they were also reading science fiction stories for Reading. By relating these two subjects in the classroom, it became easier for students to make that connection. Because science fiction is such a specific genre, we highly recommend tying the two together to help students along with their writing.

How to Evaluate the Pre-writing

The pre-writing is worth 5 points. That breaks down to 1 point for each element that is properly clustered or outlined according to the questions provided on the rubric.

How to Evaluate the Rough Draft

When evaluating the students' rough drafts, points should be assigned as follows:

a. *Followed Composition Book Guidelines* (10 points): 1 point for following each guideline.

b. *Had a clear beginning, middle, and end* (10 points): beginning (3 points), middle (4 points), and end (3 points). Give students points based on how well each part is developed.

c. *Included science fiction story elements* (10 points): on a scale of 1 to 10, how well was the story written as a science fiction narrative, and did it include appropriate story elements?

d. *Contained at least 300 words* (10 points): deduct 1 point for every ten words below 300.

When students turn in their rough drafts, they should use their class time to begin work on their book covers, title pages, and dedication pages. They could also use this time to make decisions on how they are going to "bind" and publish their books. This provides the students with plenty to do while you have their composition books for grading and conferencing.

How to Evaluate the Final Draft

When evaluating the students' final drafts, points should be assigned as follows:

a. *Used correct spelling, punctuation, and grammar* (10 points): spelling (3 points), punctuation (4 points), and grammar (3 points).

b. *Corrections from conference were made* (10 points): on a scale of 1 to 10, how well did the student make the revisions discussed during your conference?

c. *Published in book format: cover, title page, dedication page, and story* (10 points): 2 points for each requirement and 2 points for having it in the correct order.

d. *Included illustrations, drawn to your best ability, on every page* (10 points): on a scale of 1 to 10, were there illustrations on every page, and were they neat and carefully drawn?

e. *Was neat and easy to read; care was taken in publication* (10 points): on a scale of 1 to 10, was the final copy neat, easy to read, and typed or written in cursive (in black or blue ink only)?

Modifying the Rubric

We were involved in a thematic study of the solar system when we required students to write this assignment. As a result, many of our students' stories were written with an outer space aspect. Regardless of whether you teach in elementary or middle school, this assignment could be tied to whatever the students are learning in science. If you teach in middle school, collaborate with your science teachers to find out what they are studying, and require students to tie their stories in to the particular science strand they are focusing on: biology, anatomy, chemistry, geology, earth science, or environmental science. Brainstorm with students for possible directions that their stories could go on these different topics.

It is important to remember that anything you require the students to do must be stated in the rubric. Therefore, the points and requirements would have to be adjusted.

Name: _____

SCIENCE FICTION RUBRIC

Science fiction is made up of stories that often tell about science and technology of the future. These stories combine scientific fact and fiction. Many times there are specific problems the characters face and must try to solve. Be sure to include these elements when you write your science fiction story. There are five steps you will need to complete for this writing assignment. They are:

1. <u>Pre-write</u>: (Worth 5 points: _____)

   Due: _____

   You must do some form of pre-writing or brainstorming to show that you have thought your story through. A good place to start is by answering the questions:

   a. When and where does the story take place? (setting)
   b. What is the problem that needs to be solved? (plot)
   c. Why is this a problem? (plot)
   d. How does the problem get solved? (plot)
   e. Who is my story about? (characters)

2. <u>Rough Draft</u>: (Worth 40 points: _____)

   Due: _____

   Your rough draft will be graded as follows:

   a. Followed Composition Book Guidelines (10 points)
   b. Had a clear beginning, middle, and end (10 points)
   c. Included science fiction story elements (10 points)
   d. Contained at least 300 words (10 points)

3. <u>Conference</u>:

   Before you begin work on your final draft, you and I must conference about your rough draft. We will discuss all the skills you used well along with skills that need improvement. We will both keep track of these skills to help measure your improvement in writing.

4. <u>Final Draft</u>: (Worth 50 points: _____)

   Due: _____

   Your final draft will be graded as follows:

a. Correct spelling, punctuation, and grammar were used (10 points)
b. Corrections from conference were made (10 points)
c. Published in book format: cover, title page, dedication page, and story (10 points)
d. Included illustrations, drawn to your best ability, on every page (10 points)
e. Neat and easy to read; care was taken in publication (10 points)

5. Presentation: (Worth 5 points: _____)

Due: _____

When presenting your science fiction story to the class, you will be graded on the following:

a. Eye contact: did you look at the audience? (1 point)
b. Volume: could the audience hear you? (1 point)
c. Clarity: could the audience understand you? (1 point)
d. Posture: were you standing straight and tall? (1 point)
e. Pride: did you sound proud of your work? (1 point)

Please cut and return the bottom portion to your teacher. Keep the top portion in your writing folder.

Science Fiction Writing Rubric

Student Contract

I understand the writing assignment for which I am responsible. I will turn in my work by the required due dates, being careful to include all mandatory components of this assignment. I understand that anything not completed in class will become homework.

Student signature: _____   Date: _____

   a. Correct spelling, punctuation, and grammar were used (10 points)
   b. Corrections from conference were made (10 points)
   c. Published in book format: cover, title page, dedication page, and story (10 points)
   d. Included illustrations, drawn to your best ability, on every page (10 points)
   e. Neat and easy to read; care was taken in publication (10 points)

5. <u>Presentation</u>: (Worth 5 points: _____)

   Due: _____

When presenting your science fiction story to the class, you will be graded on the following:

   a. Eye contact: did you look at the audience? (1 point)
   b. Volume: could the audience hear you? (1 point)
   c. Clarity: could the audience understand you? (1 point)
   d. Posture: were you standing straight and tall? (1 point)
   e. Pride: did you sound proud of your work? (1 point)

Please cut and return the bottom portion to your teacher. Keep the top portion in your writing folder.

Science Fiction Writing Rubric

Student Contract With Parent Signature

I understand the writing assignment for which I am responsible. I will turn in my work by the required due dates, being careful to include all mandatory components of this assignment. I understand that anything not completed in class will become homework.

Student signature: _____   Date: _____

I am aware of the writing assignment for which my child is responsible as well as the due dates for each part. I understand that anything not completed in class will become homework.

Parent signature: _____   Date: _____

Name: _____

SCIENCE FICTION ROUGH DRAFT GRADING RUBRIC

Followed Composition Book Guidelines .... worth 10 points: _____

Had a clear beginning, middle, and end................. worth 10 points: _____

Included science fiction story elements .... worth 10 points: _____

Contained at least 300 words................................. worth 10 points: _____

Worth 40 points: _____

Percentage/Letter Grade: _____

Name: _____

SCIENCE FICTION FINAL DRAFT
AND PRESENTATION GRADING RUBRIC

Used correct spelling, punctuation, and
grammar .... worth 10 points: _____

Corrections from conference were made................. worth 10 points: _____

Published in book format: cover, title page,
dedication page, and story..................................... worth 10 points: _____

Included illustrations on every page .... worth 10 points: _____

Neat and easy to read; care was taken in
publication .... worth 10 points: _____

Presentation:
eye contact, volume, clarity, posture, and pride...... worth 5 points: _____

Worth 55 points: _____

Percentage/Letter Grade: _____

12

Narrative

TEACHER INSTRUCTION FOR NARRATIVE RUBRIC

Suggested Timeline

	Monday	Tuesday	Wednesday	Thursday	Friday
Week 1	Introduce Rubric			Pre-write is due	
Week 2					Rough Draft is due
Week 3	Conferences	Conferences			
Week 4				Final Draft is due Presentations	Presentations

Handouts Provided for This Assignment

Narrative rubric (three pages)

Rough draft and final draft/presentation grading rubrics (one page)

Other Materials Needed

- Reference book(s) with book-making ideas (see Resource B)
- Materials for "publishing" student narratives: colored pencils or crayons, white paper, construction paper, tag board or poster board (for book covers), scissors, glue, tape, stapler, and so on.

Introducing the Rubric

The first day of the four-week project should be spent introducing the rubric. Read it aloud to the class section by section, answering any questions the students may have as you go along. Have students fill in the due dates for each part of the process in the space provided on the rubric. Students should also fill in the due dates for each part of the process in their assignment book calendars.

This assignment is designed to give students more freedom in determining the *GASP* (*G*enre, *A*udience, *S*ubject, and *P*urpose) of their stories. You should take some time to brainstorm with the students for possible genres and topics for this assignment. This would also be a good time to work with students on "narrowing topics" (*Six Trait Writing:* Ideas). Because this is such a general assignment, students get to explore areas of writing that they are truly interested in, which can make for some incredible stories.

How to Evaluate the Pre-writing

The pre-writing is worth 5 points. That breaks down to 1 point for each element that is properly clustered or outlined according to the questions provided on the rubric, and 1 point for including the title of the story as well.

How to Evaluate the Rough Draft

When evaluating the students' rough drafts, points should be assigned as follows:

a. *Followed Composition Book Guidelines* (10 points): 1 point for following each guideline.

b. *Had a clear and well-developed plot* (10 points): on a scale of 1 to 10, how clear was the plot, and how well was it developed?

c. *Made sense and was told in a logical order* (10 points): on a scale of 1 to 10, how well did the narrative make sense, and was it told in a logical order?

d. *Contained at least 250 words* (10 points): deduct 2 points for every ten words below 250.

When students turn in their rough drafts, they should use their class time to begin work on their book covers, title pages, and dedication pages. They could also use this time to make decisions on how they are going to "bind" and publish their books. This provides the students with plenty to do while you have their composition books for grading and conferencing.

How to Evaluate the Final Draft

When evaluating the students' final drafts, points should be assigned as follows:

a. *Used correct spelling, punctuation, and grammar* (10 points): spelling (3 points), punctuation (4 points), and grammar (3 points).

b. *Corrections from conference were made* (10 points): on a scale of 1 to 10, how well did the student make the revisions discussed during your conference?

c. *Published in book format: cover, title page, dedication page, and narrative* (10 points): 2 points for each requirement and 2 points for having it in the correct order.

d. *Included illustrations, drawn to your best ability, on every page* (10 points): on a scale of 1 to 10, were there illustrations on every page, and were they neat and carefully drawn?

e. *Was neat and easy to read; care was taken in publication* (10 points): on a scale of 1 to 10, was the final copy neat, easy to read, and typed or written in cursive (in black or blue ink only)?

Modifying the Rubric

As we stated earlier, this assignment is intended to give the students more choice and freedom in determining the GASP of their projects. However, if you wanted to be more specific, you could state what any one (or all) of the requirements should be (genre, audience, subject, or purpose). It is important to remember that anything you expect the students to do must be stated in the rubric. Therefore, the points and requirements would have to be adjusted.

STUDENT EXAMPLES

Excerpts From Carly Cloud's Narrative, "Just Born"

One day, in the ocean, Mama Beluga pushed her child to the oceans surface for its first breath of air. The baby felt the air for the first time.

"Mom," he said for the first time, "what was that we were just in?"

"That was air, Whitey."

"Mom, who's Whiteeeeee?"

"Why, that is you, honey."

Soon, Mama Beluga called Whitey to come and meet another beluga, Silver. He was just as old as Whitey.

"Whitey, meet Silver."

"Hi. My name is Whitey."

"Hi," Silver said bashfully. "My name is Silver. Can we be friends?"

Whoosh! Whitey could feel Silvers spray of mist.

Brr, brr, brrooo! An engine! "A boat! My mom told me boats are dangerous."

Just then, a sperm whale appeared behind them. Pow! Whitey could taste blood.

"Hurry! Silver, we have to go before they see us!" But it was too late. They were chasing after them!

"I'm sorry we left, "Whitey said.

"It's ok. But next time listen to us, ok?"

"Yes ma'am." And Whitey and Silver began describing their adventure.

THE END

Excerpts From Molly Espinoza's Narrative, "Life Is Like the Breeze"

. . . . When we got there all the girls were heading into different classes. It was as if they had seen us coming and ran away. Behind me dragged Margaret. She was like a spider. If you got trapped in her web you couldn't get out, unless you did whatever she said.

I walked her to her classroom and she dashed in. Before I went into my first class I listened in at the door. I heard Mrs. Stanley explain a history lesson. She sounded like a leader explaining his plan to his fellow mates. Then I heard her write on the board. I crept in and slid into my seat. Without turning she said in a cold voice, "Glad you could make it Miss Morris."

The other girls began snickering. They sounded like mice. And that's the way it was, with math and geography as well. . . .

Then Mavis walked past me and slipped a note into my pocket. When I opened the note she had written "FAT CHANCE." I wrinkled my face as if I had tasted a lemon, but Sara coaxed me on.

Every night we would go for walks on the beach. The air is so strong I can almost taste it. As I sit here I think of this. Perhaps I shall write again. Perhaps you shall hear. Perhaps.

THE END

Name: _____

NARRATIVE RUBRIC

Your next writing assignment will be to compose your own story. It can be fiction or non-fiction (an actual experience you encountered). You get to determine the **GASP** of this project. There are five steps you will need to complete for this writing assignment. They are:

    1. <u>Pre-write</u>: (Worth 5 points: _____)

        Due: _____

You must do some form of pre-writing or brainstorming to show that you have thought your story through. A good place to start is by answering the questions:

        a. When and where does the story take place? (setting)
        b. What is going to happen? (plot)
        c. Is there a problem that needs to be solved? (plot)
        d. Who is my story about? (characters)

Be sure to include the title of your story on your pre-writing plan.

    2. <u>Rough Draft</u>: (Worth 40 points: _____)

        Due: _____

Your rough draft will be graded as follows:

        a. Followed Composition Book Guidelines (10 points)
        b. Had a clear and well-developed plot (10 points)
        c. Made sense and was told in a logical order (10 points)
        d. Contained at least 250 words (10 points)

    3. <u>Conference</u>:

Before you begin work on your final draft, you and I must conference about your rough draft. We will discuss all the skills you used well along with skills that need improvement. We will both keep track of these skills to help measure your improvement in writing.

    4. <u>Final Draft</u>: (Worth 50 points: _____)

        Due: _____

Your final draft will be graded as follows:

    a. Correct spelling, punctuation, and grammar were used (10 points)

    b. Corrections from conference were made (10 points)

    c. Published in book format: cover, title page, dedication page, and story (10 points)

    d. Included illustrations, drawn to your best ability, on every page (10 points)

    e. Neat and easy to read; care was taken in publication (10 points)

5. <u>Presentation:</u> (Worth 5 points: _____)

    Due: _____

When presenting your story to the class, you will be graded on the following:

    a. Eye contact: did you look at the audience? (1 point)

    b. Volume: could the audience hear you? (1 point)

    c. Clarity: could the audience understand you? (1 point)

    d. Posture: were you standing straight and tall? (1 point)

    e. Pride: did you sound proud of your work? (1 point)

Please cut and return the bottom portion to your teacher. Keep the top portion in your writing folder.

Narrative Writing Rubric

Student Contract

I understand the writing assignment for which I am responsible. I will turn in my work by the required due dates, being careful to include all mandatory components of this assignment. I understand that anything not completed in class will become homework.

Student signature: _____   Date: _____

a. Correct spelling, punctuation, and grammar were used (10 points)
b. Corrections from conference were made (10 points)
c. Published in book format: cover, title page, dedication page, and story (10 points)
d. Included illustrations, drawn to your best ability, on every page (10 points)
e. Neat and easy to read; care was taken in publication (10 points)

5. Presentation: (Worth 5 points: _____)

Due: _____

When presenting your story to the class, you will be graded on the following:

a. Eye contact: did you look at the audience? (1 point)
b. Volume: could the audience hear you? (1 point)
c. Clarity: could the audience understand you? (1 point)
d. Posture: were you standing straight and tall? (1 point)
e. Pride: did you sound proud of your work? (1 point)

Please cut and return the bottom portion to your teacher. Keep the top portion in your writing folder.

Narrative Writing Rubric

Student Contract With Parent Signature

I understand the writing assignment for which I am responsible. I will turn in my work by the required due dates, being careful to include all mandatory components of this assignment. I understand that anything not completed in class will become homework.

Student signature: _____   Date: _____

I am aware of the writing assignment for which my child is responsible as well as the due dates for each part. I understand that anything not completed in class will become homework.

Parent signature: _____   Date: _____

Name: _____

NARRATIVE ROUGH DRAFT GRADING RUBRIC

Followed Composition Book Guidelines.................worth 10 points: _____

Had a clear and well-developed plot.....................worth 10 points: _____

Made sense and was told in a logical order ....worth 10 points: _____

Contained at least 250 words................................worth 10 points: _____

Worth 40 points: _____

Percentage/Letter Grade: _____

Name: _____

NARRATIVE FINAL DRAFT AND
PRESENTATION GRADING RUBRIC

Used correct spelling, punctuation, and
grammar... worth 10 points: _____

Corrections from conference were made .... worth 10 points: _____

Published in book format: cover, title page,
dedication page, and story .... worth 10 points: _____

Included neat and carefully drawn illustrations on
every page... worth 10 points: _____

Neat and easy to read; care was taken in
publication.. worth 10 points: _____

Presentation:
eye contact, volume, clarity, posture, and pride...... worth 5 points: _____

Worth 55 points: _____

Percentage/Letter Grade: _____

13

Family Tradition

TEACHER INSTRUCTION
FOR FAMILY TRADITION RUBRIC

Suggested Timeline

	Monday	Tuesday	Wednesday	Thursday	Friday
Week 1	Introduce Rubric			Pre-write is due	
Week 2					Rough Draft is due
Week 3	Conferences	Conferences			
Week 4				Final Draft is due Presentations	Presentations

Handouts Provided for This Assignment

Family tradition rubric (three pages)

Rough draft and final draft/presentation grading rubrics (one page)

Other Materials Needed

- Reference book(s) with book-making ideas (see Resource B)
- Materials for "publishing" student tradition stories: colored pencils or crayons, white paper, construction paper, tag board or poster board (for book covers), scissors, glue, tape, stapler, and so on.

Introducing the Rubric

The first day of the four-week project should be spent introducing the rubric. Read it aloud to the class section by section, answering any questions the students may have as you go along. Have students fill in the due dates for each part of the process in the space provided on the rubric. Students should also fill in the due dates for each part of the process in their assignment book calendars.

Our favorite time to give this assignment was prior to the winter break while we were involved in a unit of study on holiday traditions celebrated throughout the world. Because we were involved in a study of traditions, students were already familiar with what they were. If this was the first time you were introducing this topic to the students, it would be important to take some time to discuss and define *traditions* with them prior to working on the assignment.

This is another assignment in which students may need help in narrowing the topic. We required the students to focus on *one* special activity or event that they participated in year after year with their families (immediate or extended), for example, the tradition of baking cookies with grandma, trimming the tree, or lighting the candles for Hanukkah. Younger students, or those with less experience in writing, had more difficulty staying focused on just one tradition. They wanted to write about everything that happened on the holiday they celebrated. We found it helpful to share some examples of the holiday traditions our family celebrated, taking time to clarify how to focus on just one event.

When going over the rough draft portion of the rubric, explain to the students that you will be going into more detail throughout the week on how to include vivid descriptions in their stories and how to appeal to the reader's senses. The way we preferred to go over descriptive language (word choice, figures of speech, sensory detail, etc.) was through our *ASAP Time* (*A*ssignments, *S*kills, *A*nd *P*roofreading) (see Chapter 2). We created our own sentences in the forms of similes, metaphors, personification, and hyperboles (students were required to label what type of figure of speech they were). We also created sentences that exemplified how to show an experience rather than just tell about it by using the senses to describe the event. By covering these skills during ASAP Time, we were reinforcing daily how to incorporate descriptive language into their own writing. In a sense, we were giving daily mini-lessons on the writing element of "word choice."

How to Evaluate the Pre-writing

The pre-writing is worth 5 points. That breaks down to 1 point for each element that is properly clustered or outlined according to the questions provided on the rubric.

How to Evaluate the Rough Draft

When evaluating the students' rough drafts, points should be assigned as follows:

   a. *Followed Composition Book Guidelines* (10 points): 1 point for following each guideline.

   b. *Included vivid descriptions; appealed to the senses* (10 points): on a scale of 1 to 10, how well was the story written with vivid description and sensory detail?

   c. *Made sense and was told in a logical order* (10 points): on a scale of 1 to 10, how well did the story make sense, and was it told in a logical order?

   d. *Contained at least 250 words* (10 points): deduct 2 points for every ten words below 250.

When students turn in their rough drafts, they should use their class time to begin work on their book covers. They could also use this time to make decisions on how they are going to "bind" and publish their books (in a creative manner). This provides the students with plenty to do while you have their composition books for grading and conferencing.

How to Evaluate the Final Draft

When evaluating the students' final drafts, points should be assigned as follows:

   a. *Used correct spelling, punctuation, and grammar* (10 points): spelling (3 points), punctuation (4 points), and grammar (3 points).

   b. *Corrections from conference were made* (10 points): on a scale of 1 to 10, how well did the student make the revisions discussed during your conference?

   c. *Published in a creative manner* (10 points): on a scale of 1 to 10, how creative was the student in publishing the story? Did the student do something different or unique that would make his or her book stand out?

    d. *Included illustrations (drawn to your best ability) or actual pictures on every page* (10 points): on a scale of 1 to 10, were there illustrations or pictures on every page, and were the illustrations neat and carefully drawn?

    e. *Was neat and easy to read; care was taken in publication* (10 points): on a scale of 1 to 10, was the final copy neat, easy to read, and typed or written in cursive (in black or blue ink only)?

Modifying the Rubric

An alternative to having students write about one of their own family traditions would be to have them interview a parent or grandparent about a tradition they experienced as a child. It is important to remember that anything you require the students to do must be stated in the rubric. Therefore, the points and requirements would have to be adjusted.

Name: _____

FAMILY TRADITION WRITING RUBRIC

For your next writing assignment, you will be working on publishing a story about your favorite family tradition. Be descriptive in your story telling. The audience should be able to clearly visualize everything you describe. There are five steps you will need to complete for this writing assignment. They are:

1. Pre-write: (Worth 5 points: _____)

   Due: _____

   A good place to start is by answering the questions:

   a. What is the tradition?
   b. Who participates in it?
   c. When and where does the tradition take place?
   d. Why do you enjoy it?
   e. How did the tradition get started?

2. Rough Draft: (Worth 40 points: _____)

   Due: _____

   Your rough draft will be graded as follows:

   a. Followed Composition Book Guidelines (10 points)
   b. Included vivid descriptions; appealed to the senses (10 points)
   c. Made sense and was told in a logical order (10 points)
   d. Contained at least 250 words (10 points)

3. Conference:

   Before you begin work on your final draft, you and I must conference about your rough draft. We will discuss all the skills you used well along with skills that need improvement. We will both keep track of these skills to help measure your improvement in writing.

4. Final Draft: (Worth 50 points: _____)

   Due: _____

   Your final draft will be graded as follows:

   a. Correct spelling, punctuation, and grammar were used (10 points)
   b. Corrections from conference were made (10 points)

    c. Published in a creative manner (10 points)

    d. Included illustrations (drawn to the best of your ability) or actual pictures on every page (10 points)

    e. Neat and easy to read; care was taken in publication (10 points)

5. <u>Presentation</u>: (Worth 5 points: _____)

    Due: _____

When presenting your story to the class, you will be graded on the following:

    a. Eye contact: did you look at the audience? (1 point)

    b. Volume: could the audience hear you? (1 point)

    c. Clarity: could the audience understand you? (1 point)

    d. Posture: were you standing straight and tall? (1 point)

    e. Pride: did you sound proud of your work? (1 point)

Please cut and return the bottom portion to your teacher. Keep the top portion in your writing folder.

Family Tradition Writing Rubric

Student Contract

I understand the writing assignment for which I am responsible. I will turn in my work by the required due dates, being careful to include all mandatory components of this assignment. I understand that anything not completed in class will become homework.

Student signature: _____   Date: _____

    c. Published in a creative manner (10 points)
    d. Included illustrations (drawn to the best of your ability) or actual pictures on every page (10 points)
    e. Neat and easy to read; care was taken in publication (10 points)

5. <u>Presentation</u>: (Worth 5 points: _____)

    Due: _____

When presenting your story to the class, you will be graded on the following:

    a. Eye contact: did you look at the audience? (1 point)
    b. Volume: could the audience hear you? (1 point)
    c. Clarity: could the audience understand you? (1 point)
    d. Posture: were you standing straight and tall? (1 point)
    e. Pride: did you sound proud of your work? (1 point)

Please cut and return the bottom portion to your teacher. Keep the top portion in your writing folder.

Family Tradition Writing Rubric

Student Contract With Parent Signature

I understand the writing assignment for which I am responsible. I will turn in my work by the required due dates, being careful to include all mandatory components of this assignment. I understand that anything not completed in class will become homework.

Student signature: _____ Date: _____

I am aware of the writing assignment for which my child is responsible as well as the due dates for each part. I understand that anything not completed in class will become homework.

Parent signature: _____ Date: _____

Name: _____

FAMILY TRADITION ROUGH DRAFT GRADING RUBRIC

Followed Composition Book Guidelines................ worth 10 points: _____

Included vivid descriptions; appealed to the
senses... worth 10 points: _____

Made sense and was told in a logical order .... worth 10 points: _____

Contained at least 250 words................................ worth 10 points: _____

Worth 40 points: _____

Percentage/Letter Grade: _____

Name: _____

FAMILY TRADITION FINAL DRAFT
AND PRESENTATION GRADING RUBRIC

Used correct spelling, punctuation, and
grammar.. worth 10 points: _____

Corrections from conference were made.................. worth 10 points: _____

Published in a creative manner .... worth 10 points: _____

Included illustrations or actual pictures on every
page .... worth 10 points: _____

Neat and easy to read; care was taken in
publication... worth 10 points: _____

Presentation:
eye contact, volume, clarity, posture, and
pride.. worth 5 points: _____

Worth 55 points: _____

Percentage/Letter Grade: _____

14

Personal Experience

TEACHER INSTRUCTION FOR PERSONAL EXPERIENCE RUBRIC

Suggested Timeline

	Monday	Tuesday	Wednesday	Thursday	Friday
Week 1	Introduce Rubric			Pre-write is due	
Week 2					Rough Draft is due
Week 3	Conferences	Conferences			
Week 4				Final Draft is due Presentations	Presentations

Handouts Provided for This Assignment

Personal experience rubric (three pages)

Rough draft and final draft/presentation grading rubrics (one page)

Other Materials Needed

- Reference book(s) with book-making ideas (see Resource B)
- Materials for "publishing" stories: colored pencils or crayons, white paper, construction paper, tag board or poster board (for book covers), scissors, glue, tape, stapler, and so on.

Introducing the Rubric

The first day of the four-week project should be spent introducing the rubric. Read it aloud to the class section by section, answering any questions the students may have as you go along. Have students fill in the due dates for each part of the process in the space provided on the rubric. Students should also fill in the due dates for each part of the process in their assignment book calendars.

When going over the rough draft portion of the rubric, explain to the students that you will be going into more detail throughout the week on how to include vivid descriptions in their stories and how to appeal to the reader's senses. The way we preferred to go over descriptive language (word choice, figures of speech, sensory detail, etc.) was through our *ASAP Time* (*A*ssignments, *S*kills, *A*nd *P*roofreading) (see Chapter 2). We created our own sentences in the forms of similes, metaphors, personification, and hyperboles (students were required to label what type of figure of speech they were). We also created sentences that exemplified how to show an experience rather than just tell about it by using the senses to describe the event. By covering these skills during ASAP Time, we were reinforcing daily how to incorporate descriptive language into their own writing. In a sense, we were giving daily mini-lessons on the writing element of "word choice."

How to Evaluate the Pre-writing

The pre-writing is worth 5 points. That breaks down to 1 point for each of the five senses that is properly clustered or outlined.

How to Evaluate the Rough Draft

When evaluating the students' rough drafts, points should be assigned as follows:

a. *Followed Composition Book Guidelines* (10 points): 1 point for following each guideline.

b. *Included vivid descriptions; appealed to the senses* (10 points): on a scale of 1 to 10, how well was the story written with vivid description and sensory detail?

c. *Made sense and was told in a logical order* (10 points): on a scale of 1 to 10, how well did the story make sense, and was it told in a logical order?

d. *Contained at least 250 words* (10 points): deduct 2 points for every ten words below 250.

When students turn in their rough drafts, they should use their class time to begin work on their book covers. They could also use this time to make decisions on how they are going to "bind" and publish their books (in a creative manner). This provides the students with plenty to do while you have their composition books for grading and conferencing.

How to Evaluate the Final Draft

When evaluating the students' final drafts, points should be assigned as follows:

a. *Used correct spelling, punctuation, and grammar* (10 points): spelling (3 points), punctuation (4 points), and grammar (3 points).

b. *Corrections from conference were made* (10 points): on a scale of 1 to 10, how well did the student make the revisions discussed during your conference?

c. *Published in a creative manner* (10 points): on a scale of 1 to 10, how creative was the student in publishing the story? Did the student do something different or unique that would make his or her book stand out?

d. *Included illustrations (drawn to your best ability) or actual pictures, on every page* (10 points): on a scale of 1 to 10, were there illustrations or pictures on every page, and were the illustrations neat and carefully drawn?

e. *Was neat and easy to read; care was taken in publication* (10 points): on a scale of 1 to 10, was the final copy neat, easy to read, and typed or written in cursive (in black or blue ink only)?

Modifying the Rubric

This writing assignment provides the students with a choice in determining their own topic. If you were interested in being more specific, you could easily determine a topic for the class. For example, you might specify that they write about an experience they had on any of the following topics:

Summer vacation, winter break, or spring break

A play or musical they attended

A museum or art gallery they visited

A travel experience: airplane, cruise, bus, car, or train

A great place they visited

A class field trip that made an impact on them

An experience focusing on one of the Character Counts traits

It is important to remember that anything you require the students to do must be stated in the rubric. Therefore, the points and requirements would have to be adjusted.

STUDENT EXAMPLES

Excerpts From Molly Espinoza's Personal Experience, "Kat's Christmas"

"Kat, you almost ready?" mom called. Kat and her family were going to the airport to pick up her Aunt Cathy and her cousin Cara. Everyone was excited. Mom was bustling about trying to find her pearl earring, Jon was looking for a leather string to pull his hair up, Sara was running after baby Ian because baby Ian had taken her cane, and Kat's room-mate and step-sister Marie was looking around for a particular head band.

Just then a loud crash came from the living room. Ian had accidently hit the Christmas Tree and it had fallen over. Everyone ran into the living room. Mom snatched the cane while Marie and Jon put the tree back up. No one was hurt though Ian was scolded severly.

Mom couldn't find her pearl earring but satisfied herself with gold studs. Jon ended up using a rubber band and Marie had to pull her hair up. When everybody was in the van mom forgot her keys and Jon needed his wallet. When they went back inside everyone began to talk at once. . . .

In the morning Kat was the first one up. She yawned and looked out the window. There was snow! "It's Christmas!" Kat shouted. She grabbed the stockings and passed them out. . . . Aunt Cathy nearly died when she saw Kat's present. She began crying. We all laughed. They gathered by the piano and Sara played "We wish you a merry Christmas and a happy new. . . ."

CRASH!

"IAN!"

Name: _____

PERSONAL EXPERIENCE WRITING RUBRIC

For your next writing assignment, you will be writing a descriptive piece about an actual event or experience you have had. You are to bring your experience to life for your readers so that they feel as though they were there with you. There are five steps you will need to complete for this writing assignment. They are:

1. <u>Pre-write</u>: (Worth 5 points: _____)

   Due: _____

Your pre-writing should be done in a form that shows what descriptions you will be including. What did you see, hear, smell, taste, and feel? Is there any other information you think is important to include? Be sure to include the event you are writing about in your title.

2. <u>Rough Draft</u>: (Worth 40 points: _____)

   Due: _____

Your rough draft will be graded as follows:

   a. Followed Composition Book Guidelines (10 points)
   b. Included vivid descriptions; appealed to the senses (10 points)
   c. Made sense and was told in a logical order (10 points)
   d. Contained at least 250 words (10 points)

3. <u>Conference</u>:

Before you begin work on your final draft, you and I must conference about your rough draft. We will discuss all the skills you used well along with skills that need improvement. We will both keep track of these skills to help measure your improvement in writing.

4. <u>Final Draft</u>: (Worth 50 points: _____)

   Due: _____

Your final draft will be graded as follows:

   a. Correct spelling, punctuation, and grammar were used (10 points)
   b. Corrections from conference were made (10 points)
   c. Published in a creative manner (10 points)

    d. Included illustrations or actual pictures on every page (10 points)

    e. Neat and easy to read; care was taken in publication (10 points)

5. <u>Presentation</u>: (Worth 5 points: _____)

    Due: _____

When presenting your story to the class, you will be graded on the following:

    a. Eye contact: did you look at the audience?

    b. Volume: could the audience hear you?

    c. Clarity: could the audience understand you?

    d. Posture: were you standing straight and tall?

    e. Pride: did you sound proud of your work?

Please cut and return the bottom portion to your teacher. Keep the top portion in your writing folder.

Personal Experience Writing Rubric

Student Contract

I understand the writing assignment for which I am responsible. I will turn in my work by the required due dates, being careful to include all mandatory components of this assignment. I understand that anything not completed in class will become homework.

Student signature: _____ Date: _____

d. Included illustrations or actual pictures on every page (10 points)

e. Neat and easy to read; care was taken in publication (10 points)

5. <u>Presentation</u>: (Worth 5 points: _____)

Due: _____

When presenting your story to the class, you will be graded on the following:

a. Eye contact: did you look at the audience?

b. Volume: could the audience hear you?

c. Clarity: could the audience understand you?

d. Posture: were you standing straight and tall?

e. Pride: did you sound proud of your work?

Please cut and return the bottom portion to your teacher. Keep the top portion in your writing folder.

Personal Experience Writing Rubric

Student Contract With Parent Signature

I understand the writing assignment for which I am responsible. I will turn in my work by the required due dates, being careful to include all mandatory components of this assignment. I understand that anything not completed in class will become homework.

Student signature: _____ Date: _____

I am aware of the writing assignment for which my child is responsible as well as the due dates for each part. I understand that anything not completed in class will become homework.

Parent signature: _____ Date: _____

Name: _____

PERSONAL EXPERIENCE ROUGH DRAFT GRADING RUBRIC

Followed Composition Book Guidelines .... worth 10 points: _____

Included vivid descriptions; appealed to the
senses .... worth 10 points: _____

Made sense and was told in a logical order .... worth 10 points: _____

Contained at least 250 words .... worth 10 points: _____

Worth 40 points: _____

Percentage/Letter Grade: _____

Name: _____

PERSONAL EXPERIENCE FINAL DRAFT
AND PRESENTATION GRADING RUBRIC

Used correct spelling, punctuation, and
grammar .... worth 10 points: _____

Corrections from conference were made .... worth 10 points: _____

Published in a creative manner .... worth 10 points: _____

Included illustrations or actual pictures on every
page .... worth 10 points: _____

Neat and easy to read; care was taken in
publication .... worth 10 points: _____

Presentation:
eye contact, volume, clarity, posture, and
pride .... worth 5 points: _____

Worth 55 points: _____

Percentage/Letter Grade: _____

PART III

Creating and Adapting Your Own Rubrics

15

How to Create Your Own Rubrics

The format of our rubrics stays basically the same for any writing assignment. If you follow this same structure, you can easily create your own rubrics for any genre of writing that you would like your students to explore. You will notice that our pre-writing and presentation grades are always worth 5 points. That leaves 90 points of the writing assignment to be divided between the rough draft and final draft. We typically assigned 40 to 50 points for each one, depending on the effort required of the students, as well as the criteria stated for each part of the process.

When you are creating your own rubrics, think backwards while planning your project. First of all, what genre of writing would you like the students to explore? What skills, elements, traits, and so on do you want the students to focus on when writing the assignment? Is there a particular format (class book, illustrated storybook, etc.) you wish the students to publish it in? Are there any other visuals (diagrams, posters, illustrations, maps, etc.) you would like the students to include during the presentations of their final drafts? If so, what type? The answers to these questions are the requirements you would include on the actual rubric.

Your next step would be to plan mini-lessons that focus on the skills you would like the students to implement. After that, you would need to either find or create reproducible pages or overheads to help illustrate these skills. Textbooks can be a great resource for such skill-building activities.

Also, be sure to plan a time frame (three to five weeks) that is appropriate for what you want to accomplish, and set the due dates accordingly. Creating your own rubrics is as simple as that!

Maintain the format we have provided for you:

Pre-write (5 points)

Rough draft (50/40 points)

Conference

Final draft (40/50 points)

Presentation (5 points)

Plan backwards:

Determine the genre

Determine the skills, elements, and traits you want to cover

    Plan mini-lessons to focus on these

    Create reproducible pages to help illustrate these

State your expectations on the rubric

Plan an appropriate time frame and set due dates accordingly

16

Adapting Our Program Across Ability Levels

As we have stated before, a great advantage in using our program is that it works so well with students of all abilities. With a few adaptations or adjustments, these rubrics can be used not only in upper elementary and middle school classrooms but in high school, special education, ESL, and gifted programs as well. Because they are designed to work with students at their ability levels, there are only a few requirements you might have to change in order to adapt these to the students with whom you are working.

HIGH SCHOOL

We have had many people comment to us about how helpful our time management instruction would be for students in high school. That, along with the format of our essay and research paper assignments, is ideal (and necessary) for students in high school to learn. Unfortunately, many teachers in elementary and middle schools do not teach students these skills and formats, which are essential for writing success in high school and beyond.

To adapt our rubrics for use in high school, minor modifications could easily be made. The essay and research rubrics could be used over and over by simply changing what you expect from the students. For example, the format for a five-paragraph essay remains the same, but the possibilities of topic choices are endless. You would also expect more from students at a high school level regarding the length of the assignment (how many words it should contain). The skills you would focus on with them would certainly be more complex than those required of elementary or middle school students. More emphasis could be placed on creative introductions and conclusions; developing their style or voice; smooth transitions between paragraphs; and sentence complexity, variety, or parallel structure. High school students may not need as much time for the assignment as well (although I would not recommend spending less than four weeks on the research paper, especially if the assignment is done primarily as homework as opposed to in class). With these few changes in expectations, our rubrics could easily be adapted for use in any high school classroom.

SPECIAL EDUCATION

The adjustments necessary for use with special education are also minor. The only real changes you might need to make to the rubrics are ones stating the length of the assignment (listing a fewer number of words required), how many resources and note cards are expected (as with the research paper), simplifying the skills you are focusing on, or providing these students with more time to complete the project. Just about everything else could remain the same. Because you work with students based on their abilities, this type of writing instruction is ideal for students with special needs.

ESL STUDENTS

We have had students in our classrooms who did not speak fluent English because they were learning it as a second language. These students were still given the same assignment, but were allowed to work through the process in their native language first. Once they had done this, they worked with their ESL teachers in translating it to English. Depending on the ESL student's ability, minor adjustments to word count requirements and so on could be made as needed.

GIFTED PROGRAMS

Our gifted students excelled with this type of writing instruction. We were often able to work with these students on more complex structure and writing elements than with other students in the class. One way to adapt these rubrics for use in a gifted program would be to use these contracts in the form of a Writer's Workshop. Provide the students with a list of all the genres they can choose from, and let them pick and choose which ones they want to work on, requiring that they complete so many rubric assignments in a grading period, or so many genres throughout the course of the year. They could also take a more active role in determining the time frame needed for them to complete the assignment. In providing students with these choices, they are given more freedom in choosing the genres and topics of their assignments, while still getting the instruction on form and framework necessary for them as well.

Resource A

Teacher-Reproducible Pages
for Composition Books

Composition Book Guidelines

* Put the date on each assignment (pre-write and rough draft)

* Keep your Table of Contents updated

* Identify your **G**enre, **A**udience, **S**ubject (topic), and **P**urpose (**GASP**) on your pre-write and rough draft

* Write in pencil, blue or black ink only

* Skip lines on your rough draft

* Write legibly

* Self-edit using your Editing Checklist and Proofreading Marks, and a red pen only

* Do not erase, simply cross out mistakes

* Keep all pages intact

Skills I Have Learned:

1. _____

2. _____

3. _____

4. _____

5. _____

6. _____

7. _____

8. _____

9. _____

10. _____

11. _____

12. _____

13. _____

Proofreading Marks

¶   Begin a new paragraph or indent the paragraph.

⌄   Insert a letter, word, phrase, or sentence.

⋀,   Insert a comma.

⌄" "⌄   Insert quotation marks.

⊙   Insert a period.

⌐   Take out a letter, word, phrase, or sentence.

╱   Change a capital letter to a small letter.

≡   Change a small letter to a capital letter.

sp   Check the spelling of a word.

¶ Once upon a time . . .

       was
He ⌄ named George.

We took coats ⋀ hats, and mittens with us.

⌄" "⌄
Stop!   shouted Sam.

This is my project ⊙

I made ⌐a a mistake.

He went to ⧸School.

We saw ‾karen‾.

sp
(Plese) edit your draft.

Editing Checklist

- Did I review my "Skills I Have Learned" list in the back of my composition book?
- Did I follow all the Composition Book Guidelines?
- Did I indent all my paragraphs?
- Did I spell all words correctly?
- Did I begin each sentence with a capital letter?
- Did I end each sentence with the correct punctuation?
- Did I use commas, apostrophes, quotation marks, and other punctuation correctly?
- Did I include a topic sentence and supporting details?
- Was each sentence a complete thought?
- Did I read my paper aloud to myself for clarity and variety?
  - Does it make sense?
  - Is it in the right order?
  - Does it have a variety of sentence starters?
  - Does it have sentence diversity (long and short sentences)?

Table of Contents

1. _____
2. _____
3. _____
4. _____
5. _____
6. _____
7. _____
8. _____
9. _____
10. _____
11. _____
12. _____
13. _____

Table of Contents

1. _____
2. _____
3. _____
4. _____
5. _____
6. _____
7. _____
8. _____
9. _____
10. _____
11. _____
12. _____
13. _____

168

Skills _____ **has learned**

Date/Title/Genre	Skills Used Well	Skills Learned

Resource B

Teacher Resources

FOR ASSIGNMENT BOOKS

Innisbrook School Supplies
P.O. Box 19507
Greensboro, NC 27419
business: 1-877-525-5608
fax: 1-800-742-2098
Web site: www.innisbrook.com

Premier, A School Specialty Company
Head office:
2000 Kentucky Street
Bellingham, WA 98226
business: 1-800-447-2034 (directs you to nearest regional office)
fax: 1-800-291-7811
Web site: www.premieragendas.com

FOR ASAP TIME

Vail, Neil J., and Joseph F. Papenfuss. *Daily Oral Language.* Wilmington, MA: Great Source Education Group, 2000. (Grades 1-12: lists two sentences for every day of the school year to edit for grammar and writing conventions.)

Vail, Neil J., and Joseph F. Papenfuss. *Daily Oral Language PLUS.* Wilmington, MA: Great Source Education Group, 2000. (Grades 1-8: lists sample sentences for every day of the school year, along with a weekly paragraph to edit for grammar and writing conventions. The sentences and paragraphs focus around a weekly theme.)

Write Source Development Group. *Daily Language Workouts.* Wilmington, MA: Great Source Education Group, 2000. (Grades 1-12: sentences and paragraphs focus on developing students' skills for editing and proofreading in mechanics, usage, and grammar.)

For ordering information on any of these sources call: 1-800-289-4490, or visit www.greatsource.com.

FOR BOOK-MAKING IDEAS

Bohning, Gerry, Ann Phillips, and Sandra H. Bryant. *Literature on the Move: Making and Using Pop-Ups and Lift-Flap Books.* Englewood, CO: Teacher Ideas Press, 1993.

Irvine, Joan. *How to Make Holiday Pop-Ups.* New York: Morrow Junior Books, 1996.

Irvine, Joan. *How to Make Pop-Ups.* New York: Morrow Junior Books, 1987.

Irvine, Joan. *How to Make Super Pop-Ups.* New York: Morrow Junior Books, 1992.

McCarthy, Mary, and Philip Manna. *Making Books by Hand.* Gloucester, MA: Rockport Publishers, 2000.

Reimer-Epp, Heidi, and Mary Reimer. *The Encyclopedia of Papermaking and Bookbinding.* Philadelphia: Running Press, 2002.

Stowell, Charlotte. *Step-by-Step: Making Books.* New York: Kingfisher, 1994.

Strong, Mary, and Mimi Neamen. *Writing Through Children's and Young Adult Literature.* Englewood, CO: Teacher Ideas Press, 1993.

Valenta, Barbara. *Pop-O-Mania: How to Create Your Own Pop-Ups.* New York: Dial Books for Young Readers, 1997.

FOR MORE INFORMATION ON THE WRITING PROCESS

Atwell, Nancie. *Coming to Know: Writing to Learn in the Intermediate Grades.* Portsmouth, NH: Heinemann, 1990.

Atwell, Nancie. *In the Middle: New Understandings About Writing, Reading, and Learning.* Portsmouth, NH: Boynton/Cook Publishers, 1998.

Atwell, Nancie. *In the Middle: Writing, Reading, and Learning With Adolescents.* Portsmouth, NH: Boynton/Cook Publishers, 1987.

Au, Kathryn H., Jacquelin H. Carroll, and Judith A. Scheu. *Balanced Literacy Instruction: A Teacher's Resource Book,* second edition. Norwood, MA: Christopher-Gordon Publishers, 2001.

Barr, Rebecca. *Teaching Reading and Writing in Elementary Classrooms.* New York: Longman, 1997.

Bly, Carol. *Beyond the Writers' Workshop: New Ways to Write Creative Nonfiction.* New York: Anchor Books, 2001.

Calkins, Lucy McCormick. *The Art of Teaching Writing.* Portsmouth, NH: Heinemann, 1986.

Calkins, Lucy McCormick. *The Art of Teaching Writing,* new edition. Portsmouth, NH: Heinemann, 1994.

Freeman, Marcia S. *Building a Writing Community: A Practical Guide.* Gainesville, FL: Maupin House Publishing, 1999.

Graves, Donald H., and Virginia Stuart. *Write From the Start: Tapping Your Child's Natural Writing Ability.* New York: Dutton, 1985.

Nathan, Ruth, Frances Temple, Kathleen Juntunen, and Charles Temple. *Classroom Strategies That Work: An Elementary Teacher's Guide to Process Writing.* Portsmouth, NH: Heinemann 1989.

Strong, Mary, and Mimi Neamen. *Writing Through Children's and Young Adult Literature.* Englewood, CO: Teacher Ideas Press, 1993.

Bibliography

Albuquerque Public Schools: District Core Curriculum and Scope & Sequence, Grades 3-5 and 6-8. Albuquerque, NM: Albuquerque Public Schools, 1996.

Atwell, Nancie. *In the Middle: Writing, Reading, and Learning With Adolescents.* Portsmouth, NH: Boynton/Cook Publishers, 1987.

Kemper, Dave, Ruth Nathan, and Patrick Sebranek. *Writers Express: A Handbook for Young Writers, Thinkers, and Learners.* Lexington, MA: D. C. Heath, 1995.

Kirszner, Laurie G., and Stephen R. Mandell. *The Holt Handbook,* second edition. Fort Worth, TX: Holt, Rinehart & Winston, 1989.

Lawrence, Elizabeth, and Jiny Duran-Ginn, directors of Teaching and Learning Systems. Albuquerque Public Schools: *District and State Standards Resource Guide.* Albuquerque, NM: Albuquerque Public Schools, 2002.

Nathan, Ruth, Frances Temple, Kathleen Juntunen, and Charles Temple. *Classroom Strategies That Work: An Elementary Teacher's Guide to Process Writing.* Portsmouth, NH: Heinemann Educational Books, 1989.

NCTE / IRA: Standards for the English Language Arts. National Council of Teachers of English, 1998–2001. www.ncte.org/standards/standards.shtml.

New Zealand's Style of Balanced Literacy, as observed in an elementary school in Phoenix, AZ, 1996. Part of The Learning Network (Richard C. Owens Group, www.rcowens.com).

Prall, Rhoda. English teacher at West Mesa High School (method for organizing a research paper), Albuquerque, NM, 1985.

Taylor, Colin F. *Native American Myths and Legends.* New York: Smithmark, 1994.

Index

**CORWIN
PRESS**